Dec. 1st, 2004

For dearest Helga,
In friendship, admiration & love,
From Treasa

Stars Above the Road

The Journey Inside

Treasa O'Driscoll

Stars Above the Road

PUBLISHED BY
Market House Book Co
A Division of Educare Press
PO Box 17222
Seattle, Washington 98107

Copyright © 2004 by Treasa O'Driscoll
All rights reserved. No part of the contents of this book may be reproduced or transmitted in any form or by any means without the written permission of the publisher.

Library of Congress Cataloging-in-Publication Data: 2004111207

O'Driscoll, Treasa
Stars Above the Road

ISBN 0-944638-61-9   US $19.95 Can. $26.95
Printed and bound in the United States of America.
1 2 3 4 5 6 7 8 9

Cover Design: iRonanworks

Contents

ARRIVING WHERE I STARTED 19

A SENSE OF PLACE 40

HERESIES OF TRUTH 59

TO GO FORTH SINGING 78

HOUSEHOLD NAMES 103

A LINGERING PRESENCE IN TORONTO 121

FLAMES OF THE ETERNAL 134

UNDERSTANDING THE MYSTERY 159

THE HERO WITHIN 172

ENTERING THE OVERLAP ZONE 186

EMBRACING THE DREAM 202

A SENSE OF RENEWAL 218

BIBLIOGRAPHY 239

Stars Above the Road

Acknowledgments

I am deeply grateful to Joy and Bob Kwapien for making me believe that I could write a book. Their financial support, encouragement and insight made it possible. Dr. Frieda Carmody provided a perfect setting; my parents and siblings gave the refuge of their hearts and homes when needed, my children cheered me from afar; Claude Bellin was my mainstay of wisdom and inspiration. Anne Stockton was faithful in soul friendship. On the North American side I acknowledge the generosity of Annemarie and Chris Heintz, Dr. Werner and Linda Fabian, the foresight of Helga Bosse, the technical assistance of Robin Munro and Jeff Alward. I owe a debt of gratitude to the following friends, many of whom continue to inspire and support my journey, Chuck and Diane Kyd, Diane Hogarth, Bill and Cathy Graham, Jeff and Merle Levin, Maureen Waller, Diane Hoover, Eric Lehner, Catherine Brennan, Anne McMurtry, Maura McCay, Therese Schroeder-Sheker, Victor and Rita Costanzi, Rufus Goodwin, Deirdre Maguire, Barbara Vincent, Finbar and Sophia Christine Murphy, John and Carrie Schuchardt, Steven Scotti, Professor James Flannery, Rev. Edward Jackman, Rita Lydon, Sr. Jo Tarpey, Pat and Riona Dwyer, John Fox, Dr. Gerald Kernow, Alexander Blair-Ewart,

Treasa O'Driscoll

Wendy Brown, Vince and Glada McIntyre, Jay Ramsey. In embodying the truth they profess the following teachers are a source of inspiration in their work and being: Dr. Ross Laing, Paul Price, Miha Pogacnik, Georg Kühlewind, Mark Patrick Hederman. I am grateful to James Redfield and his wife Salle for hospitality extended in Alabama and for quotations from The Tenth Insight. I thank Michael Yeats for permission to include extracts from his father's published works, Robert Sardello who allowed me to quote from his books and who was so generous in his comments on my original draft. Robert and his wife Cheryl have, as beloved mentors and colleagues, opened new vistas of understanding for me and thousands of other students of their School of Spiritual Psychology. Christopher Bamford, cherished friend and mentor has spurred me on and I thank him for permission to quote from publications of Lindisfarne Books and Anthroposophic Press. Lastly I thank my publisher Kieran O'Mahony for his faith in this project and for skillful editing.

*For my children,
Briain, Robert, Declan and Emer,
and grandchildren,
Tristan, Anwen, Tyrnan, Ilan, and others yet to come...*

I FIND MY STAR

The wishes of the soul are springing.
The deeds of the will are thriving.
The fruits of the life are maturing.
I feel my destiny.
My destiny finds me.
I feel my star.
My star finds me.
I feel my goals in life.
My goals in life are finding me.
My soul and the great world are one.
Life grows more radiant about me.
Life grows more arduous for me.
Life grows more abundant within me.
                              Rudolf Steiner

"Would you tell me please which way I ought to go from here?"
"That depends on where you want to get to," said the cat.
Lewis Carroll

One

ARRIVING WHERE I STARTED

Edging onto the tree-lined bank, I lowered the car window. "Would you please tell me the way to Killaloe?" A burly farmer easily enthroned on his tractor commanded the width of that narrow country road. I had been confounded by the choice of winding side-roads on the map, all purporting to lead to the ancient capital of Ireland, now an unpretentious town in County Clare that sits contentedly on the shores of Lough Derg.

"I would indeed," said he, as he eyed the potholes in the road. "But I wouldn't be setting out from here at all, if I were you."

He then proceeded to put me "on the right road," where presumably I could make a new beginning.

Treasa O'Driscoll

"You can start to find your way from there," was what he said in the lilting accent of the place.

I thanked him and made my way to the crossroads where a surer, somewhat wider, more evenly paved roadway stretched before me. The farmer's vigorous words echoed in my mind and gave me food for thought for the remainder of my journey. I recalled a few lines from a poem I learned as a child.

> The little roads of Ireland
> Go wandering up and down
> O'er hill and moor and valley
> By rath and tower and town.

Today, I mused, the roads of Ireland can be cited as a metaphor for modern lives caught in the swing between too much and too little. Interweaving and underpinning the sleek expressways that conduct the flow of Ireland's celebrated *Celtic Tiger* economy is a network of straggling boreens [Irish for *little roads*] replete with potholes. Because every highway inexorably gives way to a byway, drivers are compelled to adapt to the slower pace of crowded towns and narrow village streets. My country of origin also accommodates many radically individualistic points of view within its insular boundary. This stimulates the indefinable excitement that so many visitors experience when they set foot on Irish soil. In artists, this divine madness gives rise to mood swings that only the exercise of writing or painting can bring into balance. Creative energy is unleashed in the tension of highs and lows just as surely as color proceeds from the interplay of light and dark. By embracing seeming contradictions in our experience we allow unexpected elements of unity to arise in consciousness. "Without opposites there is no progression," was a favorite remark of my late husband's.

The human soul mediates eternally between poles of sympathy and antipathy, according to one of the great philosophers of the twentieth century, Rudolf Steiner, who pioneered a path of inner development and conscious soul life.

The capacity inherent in consciousness to observe, conceive and imagine, sustains the life of the soul in the whole range of its pathos and endows it with innate nobility and purpose. My life has been greatly enriched by Steiner's expanded world view that includes invisible as well as visible reality and encourages the witnessing of inner experience in oneself. When I approach the events of my own life in an experimental spirit of enquiry it enables me to create a space for freedom in my thoughts and actions. Emotional balance is all the more durable when one arrives at it by way of self-observation. Meister Eckhart made much reference to *the way of paradox*, others have termed it *the middle way*. Rainer Maria Rilke understood the importance of uniting all seeming contradiction within.

> ...Take your practiced powers
> And stretch them out
> Until they span the chasm between two contradictions
> Because the God wants to know Himself in you.

All In The Waiting

My mind tends to be at its most active while I am driving or walking, and I continued to follow my train of thought as I approached my destination of Killaloe-Ballina, twin towns joined by a narrow bridge. I had traveled from Canada and had made my way to my native land to write this book. I wanted the rich tapestry of my life to unfold its gathered wisdom because I believed that in contemplating my own biography I could achieve greater clarity and direction in my thinking. "We women are moons and we must become suns," declared my wisest woman friend in whom this transition is radiantly obvious after over ninety years of living.

I was somewhat wary of adding to the ranks of would-be authors who dazzled captive audiences in pubs around the country with outlines of plots that would drown in pints of Guinness. I knew that certain preconditions attend creative endeavor. These preconditions were clearly outlined for me by Robert Fritz whom I had encountered in Toronto many years before. A successful American composer, in his desire to probe the mysteries of creativity, he made a keen study of the process through which his completed works emerged. He discovered that inspiration was merely a starting point. Fritz's training course and book *The Path of Least Resistance* had demonstrated how I could engage the play of opposites to maximize creativity in every area of life so that I could give more practical application to my ideals. All visionary flights he cautioned, must be tempered with a cold clear look at one's *current reality*. By holding both vision and current reality in consciousness simultaneously, a structural tension is built up inwardly which invariably resolves itself in favor of the vision. In always referring to current reality one preserves entire truthfulness in regard to the circumstances of one's life however disturbing they might be, and wins the right to whatever rewards the vision may bring. I had put this technique into practice a few months before arriving in Ireland. I envisioned my book as a *fait accompli* while noting my inability to type, my lack of stable living conditions or funds. Current reality presented a very dismal picture indeed...

Holding the focus of these factors simultaneously I referred to them from time to time and entered into the spirit of T.S. Eliot's lines:

> I said to my soul, be still and wait without hope
> For hope would be hope for the wrong thing; wait without love
> For love would be love for the wrong thing; there is yet faith
> But the faith and the hope and the love are all in the waiting...

Right action in its rightful time arises out of the inner, plentiful void of an expectant waiting. Soon life began to arrange a chain of events through which an ever-changing current reality and stable vision edged closer to one another in time. As if by miracle, a friend who was also a publisher offered me an advance on my book and suggested the most ideal surroundings in the west of Ireland in which to write. I was facilitated in my growing resolve at every turn so that intense gratitude for the bounty of providence now became my daily mood of soul as I prepared for the adventure ahead...

The Way of the Mother

Eliot's words had also helped to give my life new direction in 1990 when, after considerable inner struggle, I managed to break loose from a domestic situation that had become intolerable to me. A firmly held conviction of the indissolubility of the marriage bond died hard. Although friends and family encouraged the move, I only crossed the threshold of realization one day when I finally admitted to a trusted counselor in a very small voice, "I do not want to be married anymore." Like many other women in later life who have once been timid, I felt a gathering of forces in me that enabled me to say no to a way of life that I could no longer sustain but which was a source of material security to me. Finding myself at odds with many of the events of a household that was once my pride and joy caused great upheaval in the life of my family. All order was displaced for a time as though we were living in the wake of an earthquake. The illusions and un-examined assumptions with which I began an earlier, more naive phase of my life all surfaced for review and redemption. It was not difficult to trace them retrospectively from the compromising circumstances that crowded around me and from which I now sought release.

Change intensified during the following years. A new order of life seemed intent on breaking through from within. This power was termed *menopause*. It was to be celebrated rather than deplored, for a natural shift of focus occurred as my bodily reality altered to accommodate awakening spiritual faculties and the greater expansion of my intrinsic love nature. With it came an appetite for new adventure rather in the spirit of the three Irish monks who set out from the south of Ireland sometime during the sixth century. They pushed out in their little *currach* [small boat] without benefit of oar or sail. After some time at sea they drifted ashore somewhere on the English coastline. Emerging from their frail vessel, they were questioned by an inhabitant: "Why have you come here?"

"We do not know," came the reply. "But we must be always on pilgrimage, we know not where."

So much were they imbued with an awareness of the love indwelling every human heart that they were impelled to go forth to meet as many people as possible in order to more fully live this mystery. Divine presence was *known* not simply inferred. This is how I began to know it at this time of my life. All encounters with other people seemed more than ever enchanted and sacred. I sense this realization in many women my age in the climate of freedom and changing values in which we live, charged with the potential of "that–which–is–not–yet." Some fifty million women are moving through menopause at the turn of this twenty first century. Many are imbued with conscious spiritual intent, peaceful and loving, holding the focus of a more harmonious and unified whole, to bring mankind through the proverbial eye of the needle. Ralph Waldo Emerson has expressed the essence of what many of my contemporaries realize-

> *The secret of culture is to learn that a few great points steadily reappear... and, that these few are alone to be graded: the escape from all false ties; courage to be what we are, and love of what is simple and beautiful; independence and cheerful relation, these are the essentials, these, and the wish to serve, to add something to the well-being of men and women.*

There is a mother's heart at the centre of existence whose warmth can penetrate selfishness, exploitation and apathy. It is this heart that both men and women are learning to access today. In later life when the demands of mothering and homemaking have been largely satisfied women begin to recognize a profound desire to be of service to the whole. We are entering an age of opportunity for women to become inspiring counsellors and far sighted leaders imbued with a new feminine ideal that arises out of the breakdown of the old order of analytic consciousness.

The *new feminine* calls for trust in the face of adversity, unconditional living on the edge of uncertainty, a freeing and schooling of our attention and a renewal of the imagination. Paula Brown, an American poet, gave voice to her experience of the divinity she found imminent in the company of women keeping vigil at their peace camp at Greenham Common in England. She had entered into this deepest of all hearts.

> If in time to come
> A child should ask me why...How?
> I would reply
> There came upon the earth a new Mary
> She sung songs
> She built a web
> She grew like a great flower in the light of
> Her own truth and sisterhood.
> She was the Mary of Joys and Sorrows
> She was the inward meeting of the rivers
> She was the moon and tides of ocean and blood
> She was the wound...and she was wise...
>
> From Paula Brown, *The New Mary*

The presence of this new Mary fully and sadly acknowledges the painful reality that men women, children and the old are living in abject conditions of disease, war and poverty, that forests and seas are dying, that many are condemned to homelessness and hopelessness.

As if to underscore these thoughts as I drove the winding country road to Killaloe, my attention was drawn to a large statue of *Our Blessed Virgin*, as she is fondly called here, her arms outstretched to gather in her children. Her figure commanded a stretch of road as I rounded another bend. A source of bemused speculation for scientist, skeptic and believer was a phenomenon that occurred in 1986, when no less than fifteen of these wayside statues of Mary began to perceptibly sway backwards and forwards and from side to side. I was sojourning in County Cork at the time, my place of residence located only six miles from Ballinaspittle, where the most remarkable of these phenomena could be witnessed. Kathleen Raine, England's great poet wrote, admonishing me to... *go and see if the statue is really moving. Perhaps you can determine what it is the Virgin is trying to tell us...* Each time I cycled to the spot and knelt before the roadside shrine, I could distinctly observe the movement in the statue. Paula Brown's poem, discovered when I opened a newly acquired book, was the closest I came to revelation. I knew the Virgin was drawing the attention of women everywhere to the wellspring of renewal that lies within our collective consciousness.

>We are the purpose, she said,
>The vision is us.

The source of that renewal is our acknowledgment of the presence of the Divine Mother more than ever before active in the world. We can apprehend this force of love and transformation, of which statues, pictures and concepts are but pale reminders, wherever virtue prevails. When we cultivate *Devotion, Balance, Faithfulness, Selflessness, Compassion, Courtesy, Equanimity, Patience, Truth, Courage, Discernment* and *Love* we take up the activity of soul traditionally perfected by Mary. Virtues imply a practical doing. In the practice of virtue values, ethics and morals leave the high ground of theory, where they have been marooned by dogma and find potent expression in human relationships. Virtue arises out of a reconciliation of opposites in oneself and implies hospitality towards our own negative traits. By following closely the movement from the depths to heights of our experience we develop a conscious soul life which can work against the loss of soul in the world.

Only the practice of virtue will bring us into true community with others. Before we come to community we have to know ourselves very well, to realize that our reaction to another person is an encounter with an aspect of ourselves. The quality of our relationships is an accurate measure of the degree to which we have embodied virtue. This process begins with an ability to live with one's own imperfections, in not hiding behind appearance or in clinging to habit, in being always ready to begin anew. Virtue demands the cultivation of imagination, which is no more than the ability to create images of all that we are not, that we might fulfill the potential inherent in our humanity.

The soul flourishes in this activity of engagement with the virtues. It is analogous with artistic activity in us—a treading of a middle way in our life of feeling. I find it comforting to know that it is by way of timidity and recklessness that *Courage* is born in us. Neither can one realize *Selflessness* unless one is familiar with the extent of one's own selfishness and self abnegation. As we become accustomed to the sensation of soul pleasure that the practice of virtue gives so does its activity increase in us. It is its own reward and the purpose of our life on earth. As the rose blooms so that the rest of the garden may be beautiful so patience develops in us, that *Patience* may permeate our world. If we pay attention to our daily lives we cannot fail to notice that virtue lives as the medium of all fruitful interaction with others.

In times past religious training presupposed an increase in morals. Today people engage in a variety of spiritual exercises which do not necessarily affect the moral sense. Witness the frequent falls from grace of venerated gurus, previously upheld as paragons of excellence whose exacting practices nevertheless failed in the development of any real moral fibre.

Virtue becomes the basis of a new psychology appropriate to modern consciousness. Virtue imbues us with the moral fortitude necessary to withstand the forces that oppose the spiritualization of the earth. Rilke could sense, like other intuitives, that our earth was urgently asking for its own transformation in the crucible of human hearts. We may join with him in his vigorous assent-

Earth, dear earth, I will do it!

The archetypal mother, traditionally of virgin purity, prepares our hearts for this task which requires precision in thinking and expression, in increased attention to the use and meaning of words. As I drove along this Irish road I could sense that Our Lady was calling for a re-evaluation of the appellation *Virgin* beyond its limited biological interpretation. A wider connotation of the term emerged from my reading of Rudolf Steiner's *The Fifth Gospel*. In a passage that strikes the reader with the full force of revelation, Dr. Steiner describes a meeting that took place between Jesus and his mother before the baptism in the river Jordan. Weary from his extensive travels and in deep distress at all he had witnessed of human depravity and the uneasy future that lay ahead for humanity, Jesus lays all his troubles at Mary's feet. As he unburdens himself Mary listens in the depth of her heart. Doubt leaves him and he begins to accept the fullness of the Christ impulse and the fulfillment of his teaching mission. In the intensity of their loving exchange, Mary also undergoes a transformation. Her virgin state of soul now becomes the ground for the incarnation of that being of wisdom that we identify as *Sophia*. A *virgin* in essence, is every man and woman today who cultivates purity of intent and maintains a receptiveness to the gift of wisdom, always within human reach. Our union with the being of the Mother is always a prerequisite for the renewal of love and understanding in our souls. The following words are familiar to readers of the New Testament. When I first heard them as a child they were a source of wonder to me.

> "*Mary kept all these words and pondered them in her heart.*"

Angelic Presence

Just as the biblical Mary pondered the words, one learns a poem by heart to retain it as a source of contemplation. As soon as the words are imprinted on the mind, conventional thinking about the content gives way to a more subtle awareness of the meaning that interlaces the fabric of vowels and consonants. Just as the leaves on a plant hold back their *leafing* impulse to allow blossoms to flower, so did Mary keep her counsel until the true spiritual import of words and events could reveal themselves.

> *As Mary receives the words of the angels, the words told by the shepherds, and the words of the twelve-year-old Jesus in her heart, with meditative thought, she lets their spiritual meaning emerge from them like spiritual forms. In the soul of Mary there emerges from each group of words, a spiritual butterfly.*
>
> From *Emil Boch*, Studies in the Gospels

Here we are also provided with a perfect description of what lives in the element of poetry, which has upheld that meditative mindfulness in which Mary was so accomplished. Poetry provides ground on which the spirit can rest. W.B. Yeats went so far as to say: *Only in what poets have affirmed in their finest moments have we come anywhere close to an authentic religion.*

The tenet most central to every Christian life was articulated by St. Paul; *Not I but Christ in me.* The words gained more immediacy for me when I pondered and memorized an inspired poem by D.H. Lawrence which conveys that attitude of humility and readiness which Paul's invocation implies.

> Not I, not I but the wind that blows through me!
> A fine wind is blowing the new direction of Time.
> If only I let it bear me, carry me, if only it carry me!
> If only I am sensitive, subtle, oh, delicate, a winged gift!
> If only, most lovely of all, I yield myself and am borrowed
> By the fine, fine wind, that takes its course
> Through the chaos of the world...
>
> From D. H. Lawrence, *The Song of the Man Who Has Come Through*

The mood of this poem draws angels towards Lawrence. He acknowledges their presence in the concluding lines of the poem.

Rainer Maria Rilke, out of his own loneliness and inner readiness, also experienced the overshadowing of angelic presence:

> *Who can have lived his life in solitude and not have marveled how the angels there will visit him at times and let him share what can't be given to the multitude.*

Treasa O'Driscoll

Central to the work of any poet is the commission to praise the work of the creator and to uphold the sources of imagination and creativity, as Paul Mathews points out in his book *Sing Me the Creation*. Caedmon, who lived in the seventh century, was the first English poet we know by name, a stuttering, unlettered stable hand. He took flight from the campfire when he noticed the harp was being passed to him, a sign that it was his turn to sing. He made some excuse about having to feed the animals and repaired to the barn. Falling into a deep sleep, he dreamed an angel stood before him.

> "Caedmon, sing me something," the angel said.
> "I cannot sing. I left the feasting and came here because I could not."
> "Nevertheless, you can sing to me," responded the angel.
> "What shall I sing?" questioned Caedmon.
> "Sing me the creation!" ordered the angel.

Caedmon, with the help of the angel, composed in his sleep a hymn to the creator and in the morning he knocked on the door of the nearby monastery of Whitby, where the Celtic way was upheld by the Abbess Hilda. The monks recorded his memorized poem in careful calligraphy. He later joined the monastic community and became a composer of verses on Christian themes. One assumes that the angel continued to be his muse. *Like a clean animal he ruminated and converted all into the sweetest music.* Caedmon is a *significant threshold figure*, writes Paul Mathews: *...his act of breaking the tribal circle epitomized a fundamental shift in western civilization.* Another shift is occurring today with the phenomena of *healing circles* where people gather together for artistic and therapeutic purposes and to develop a speech of the heart. Paul

Matthews is a leader in the field, actively involved in restoring the connection between the spoken and written word. He establishes circles of poetry, love and truth wherever he travels. When I met him at Emerson College in Sussex where my son Declan was his student, we acknowledged common sources of inspiration. I recognized him as one of the emerging world tribe, designated by Rudolf Steiner, *the knighthood of the Word.*

Momentum of Memory

Perhaps a similar insight had informed the Irish educational system of my youth. I left secondary school with a repertoire of memorized poems and songs, the foundation for a life long practice of *learning by heart* — my guarantee of mental well-being, and the basis of a performance career that would blossom many years later. What began as enforced learning by rote with more care for sound than sense developed into as genuine a love for the words, ideas, imagination and rhythms as my youthful capacity could muster. My mother's beautiful singing voice and her gift of rhymes and stories had taught me to listen from infancy as though the whole skin surface of my body was an attenuated ear. A mother who can sing prepares the soul of a child for poetry and forms the actual larynx of the child for musical speech and song.

When I was thirteen or so I had a conscious awakening to the miracle of speech when I encountered a remarkable teacher who had grown up with Irish as her first language in a remote area of Connemara in the west of Ireland. A person of high intellect, she had absorbed the riches of oral and written literature in the Irish language. When I heard her recite *Donal Og* the bitter remonstration of a jilted lover, its many verses describing in imaginative pictures, the searing pain of unrequited love, it was as though an arrow of truth pierced through the very center of my heart. The content was beyond my emotional comprehension at the time and yet, what remains with me is the sense of having been touched in a part of the spirit where I had not been touched before.

> For you took what's before me and what's behind me,
> You took east and west when you wouldn't mind me,
> Sun and moon from my sky you've taken,
> And God as well, or I'm much mistaken.

In Mairéad Nic Dhonncha's speaking I first understood how soul enhancing the sense of language is and how it carries through in the voice. Her way of speaking was characteristic of her place of birth, a total unity of sound and sense was natural to her, mellifluous intonation, a savoring of vowels, an appreciation of consonants, a musicality of phrasing, an ability to convey deep feeling without reverting to sentimentality or excess. The relatively small number of Irish people who still speak our native language have something in common with aborigines everywhere. As an old Eskimo woman recalled:

> *Those were the days when words were like magic. The human voice had mysterious powers. A word spoken might suddenly become alive. What people said might happen.*

Rudolf Steiner in his book *Cosmic Memory* describes how human language first came into being.

> *Among women that which lived within them could transpose itself into a kind of natural language. For the beginning of languages is something which is similar to song... The inner rhythm of nature sounded from the lips of wise women and in their songlike sentences the utterances of higher powers were felt...for at that period there can be no question of sense in that which was spoken. Sound, tone and rhythm were perceived.*

Mairéad Nic Dhonncha coached me in the interpretation of sean nós [old style] songs that are still a standard part of my repertoire. I have also dipped into the poetic continuum of east and west, choosing poems which are crafted to reveal and sustain meaning and uphold the soul's movement between self and surroundings, transforming Keats' "vale of tears" into a "vale of soulmaking."

Good poetry is born out of a reverence for life. Arising out of our powerful instinct for self preservation, the poetic tradition is a genuine source of joy and strength flowing out of our human story, transcending historical fact by virtue of its enduring qualities of beauty and truth. As soon as I am drawn into the mystery of a poem, the import of the words sink in, often appearing to express my own hidden thoughts. I will repeat the words over and over until I have made them my own, deriving great pleasure from this exercise as my appreciation for the content grows like a source of inner light and strength. This absorption with a particular poem and the subsequent performance of it becomes a rite of passage for me to a deeper level of awareness. This deepening often occurs in the presence of an audience who enter into the process of discovery with me.

Continuity

The famous Irish four-seasons-in-one-day variable was evident as I sped along the road to Killaloe, noting the extensive flooding that was such a source of distress for small farmers that year. Animals, wading through mucky and water logged fields, looked disoriented and forlorn. Due to a lack of fodder they were brought to a state of famine in some areas. Gradually the rain ceased, and the sun slanted out and soon flooding light illumined a desolate landscape. Approaching a lay-by that overlooked the beautiful Shannon River I stopped the car to admire the play of light on calm waters. Retrieving a notebook from my handbag I jotted down some of the thoughts the journey had afforded me. I had a definite sense that I was coming home—I was now only a few miles from Ogonolloe which I knew to be the territory of my ancestors, Gradys and Costelloes, McNamaras, Armstrongs and Grealishs. I recalled the litany of names on my mother's lips when she spoke nostalgically of her youth in Clare. When I told her I would be living at Tinarana House my aunt's face lit up. "Your great-grandmother provided the fabric for the quilt-making that went on there years ago." To think that I would weave my tapestry of words under that same roof... I had so often talked about the continuity of tradition and how one skill metamorphosed into another between generations. Seamus Heaney's poem, *Digging*, expresses it best. In this poem he recalls his father's and grandfather's engagement in the farming activities that characterized his rural upbringing.

> ...Nicking and slicing neatly, heaving sods
> Over his shoulder, going down and down
> For the good turf, digging...

Heaney sees the analogy between the generations of diggers that went before him and his own determined harvesting of words.

> ...But I've no spade to follow men like them
> Between my finger and my thumb
> The squat pen rests.
> I'll dig with it.

We cannot all be scholars, nor can we house vast libraries of books in the hope of somehow preserving the heritage of the past. Information as to who and what we are is now being imposed on us from all sides. There is often a disturbing disassociation between all this data and the lives we actually live, a source of anxiety in itself. A poet possesses a unique capacity to select, isolate, and integrate the essence of this knowledge with metaphysical insight, for the purpose of throwing light on the perplexing condition of being human.

Destination

In Ireland past, present, and future seem woven in a timeless mantle over the events of everyday life. I enjoyed such moments of backward-forward-inward intensity as I drove through the open gateway and meandered up a driveway, past an enchanted woodland populated by red and fallow deer. Tinarana House, the imposing nineteenth century mansion that loomed behind the trees was to be my home for the months ahead. The twenty odd years spent in one house during my marriage seemed to have satisfied my need for a permanent dwelling. When that period of my life ended a need arose like a hunger or thirst, that was only satisfied by new places, books and conversation. I learned the importance of having long periods of solitude. I could enter more fully because of that into interaction with others. I knew that I could only be content with a life-style that allowed me this rhythm. A meditative approach to life, far from isolating me actually led to more intense involvement with the world. A gem of wisdom from a sixth century Irish monk, written at a time when Rome represented the pinnacle of holiness, confirms this truth.

> Who to Rome goes
> Little comfort knows
> For God on earth
> Though long you've sought Him

You'll miss in Rome
Unless you've brought Him!

And this I believe, is the secret of happiness—that elusive state of being that we relentlessly seek. We can become erroneously convinced that the experience of happiness is dependent on external circumstance or causal relationship when in fact it is self-determined. It stems I believe from a sense of one's own inner worth, independent of external circumstances. We all have flashes throughout our lives of what we term *happiness* and some distinct memories of what by contrast arises as *unhappiness*. Carlo Pietzner, an artist and spiritual teacher, suggests that there is in fact a kind of inner qualitative ladder for the experience of happiness. He describes the three stages we are all familiar with from naive foolishness through a period of doubt into the third great phase—blessedness, impersonal happiness, being in tune not only with oneself but with the world.

My fiftieth year had come and gone,
I sat, a solitary man
In a crowded London shop,
An open book and empty cup
On the marble table top.

While on the shop and street I gazed
My body of a sudden blazed;
And twenty minutes more or less
It seemed, so great my happiness,
That I was blessed and could bless.
From W.B. Yeats, Vacillation.

These are the words of a man who understands what it means to come home to his own spiritual nature. I could recall these words at will from the hundreds of lines from this poet's work I had memorized. Yeats had taken a radical path of poetry which enlivened and deepened his soul life. It was also the path of friendship. The pattern of destiny that moved through Yeats' life included collaboration with many other gifted and famous men and women of his day. I had driven past Coole Park, in County Galway, on my way to Tinarana. Once the home of Lady Gregory, it had been the location for significant meetings between her and Yeats and other writers and visionaries, a powerful stimulus for the artistic life of their time. Lady Gregory, George Hyde-Lees, Maud Gonne, James Stephens, John Millington Synge, Ezra Pound and John Quinn, had helped shape the creative genius and public interests of Yeats. His life demonstrates that fulfillment is never self-created. It must always be given by the world, by other people, by the environment, by the attuning of one's own destiny with the world, with the time and with the people with whom one lives. Each one of us has our own litany of names of those people who have contributed to the totality of who we are in thought and action and belonging. They have shown us how wholeness results from the ability to balance our own needs with the needs of others. We are each other's teachers in this experiment in the art of living and social renewal. I have learned most from those who are the most conscious in what they do and say. I write in praise of friends and mentors whose example of living has influenced mine. I wish to also demonstrate the central tenet of the life I lead; that it is the recognition of the presence of love in each individual that transforms experience into the stuff that dreams are made on.

With bated breath I knocked on the door of Tinarana House.

Treasa O'Driscoll

> *"Tory Island, Knocknarea, Slieve Patrick, all of them steeped in associations from the older culture, will not stir us beyond a usual pleasure unless that culture means something to us, unless the features of the landscape are a mode of communion with a something other than themselves, a something to which we ourselves still feel we might belong."*
> Seamus Heaney

Two

A SENSE OF PLACE

Hello, I'm Treasa—I've come to stay. I stood hesitant on the doorstep, surrounded by baggage and the chill of a January afternoon.

"Welcome. We have been expecting you," said the cheerful smiling woman who opened the door. It was heavy, yellow. All apprehension vanished and my sense was that of home-coming.

The hospitality of Clare people is legendary. My late grandmother, Bridget, was a native of this county. She told me that there was a living memory amongst her people of abject conditions that were the legacy of famine and evictions. Their own poverty notwithstanding, my forebears found ways to make a stranger feel welcome and happy. "We'll spread green rushes under your feet!"— conveyed the respect that was natural amongst them at the appearance of a visitor. There was an abundance of green rushes growing on the river banks. I can remember my mother and her friends laying them out on the kitchen floor when I was a child, in preparation for the task of plaiting them into crosses for St. Bridget's day, February 1. This tradition still continues. A Clare custom that also survived in our family was the inclusion of music and dance in every gathering. Anybody who could play a few tunes on the fiddle or piano, or dance a set was called into action as soon as refreshments were served to the guests. My Clare grandfather taught Irish dancing and was a fine flute player. He was carried off by tuberculosis before I was born like many other Irishmen of the time. It was from my mother that I inherited the gift of singing and imitated from an early age her spontaneous response to any request for a song. "Since the gift is God-given it must be shared with all," was what I was told. I imbibed the spirit of the following old rune with my mother's milk:

> I saw a stranger yesterday
> I put food for him in the eating place
> Drink for him in the drinking place
> And in the Holy name of the Trinity
> He blessed myself and my house
> My possessions and my family.
> And the lark said as she sang:
> It is often, often, often,
> Christ comes disguised
> As a stranger.
>
> Anon.

There were no rushes in sight as I crossed the threshold of the stately mansion far removed from the dirt floor hovels of famine time. An abundance of greenery and long, white lilies met my eye as I entered the reception area. A red carpet symbolically led the way along an old pitch pine stairway. The smell of burning cedar mingled with the aroma of the perfumed candles which flickered in every corner. Soft lights cast a glow on polished wood and reflected in the elegantly furnished adjoining rooms.

Shades of lives long gone seemed to hover in the twilight. In such an atmosphere as this, one might draw nearer to the old poets W.B. Yeats so often talked about, the ones who *had a seat at every hearth*, if one could only enter a condition of timelessness and allow one's own longings and aspirations to mingle with theirs.

My reverie was broken as staff members rushed forward to introduce themselves. They were few in number compared with the swell of vassals and serfs of one hundred years before, amongst whom probably numbered some of my ancestors, who scurried and scrubbed and hauled to meet the demands of a prestigious household. I was soon swept up in a whirl of welcome and well-wishing, relieved of the burden of luggage by strong and eager hands.

I was encouraged to choose my own room from amongst the vacant ones. It was early season and paying guests were few. After some careful deliberation I opted for a lovely ensuite in the attic that held the promise of solitude. It would be beyond earshot of engaging conversations and the rest of the household buzz. There were a few bookshelves in the corner and at my request a desk was placed in front of the window that afforded me a lovely view of Lough Derg that was only slightly obscured by a lattice of saplings, stark against a winter sky.

Stars Above the Road

I heard once that angels assume as their form bodies of water, and this imagination invariably causes me to look with awe at such a stretch as now spread out before me. The shimmering pearl grey surface of the lake betrayed a tremor of movement and perfectly mirrored the shade of the afternoon sky. I knew from the experience of growing up in Ireland and my frequent sojourns in stormy Connaught that before the month was out I would witness many variations on this now tranquil scene. Sudden weather changes would call wind and rain into capricious service amidst shifting cloud formations and the play of light and shadow. Slanting rays would shyly appear from behind a brightening curtain of sky to briefly highlight some new detail of the landscape. I knew that waters could stir at the blink of an eyelid from tranquil to storm shrouded turbulence. Distant hills that were at one moment cast into a reflective tableau on a polished mirror of lake could, in the next moment, present a verticality of blue and purple hue interwoven with luminous patches of mossy green or peat brown. Sometimes dense clusters of woodland would come to light against the skyline or seem to plunge down into hidden depths and form fringes of inky black around the inlets.

One could not remain indifferent to natural forces in this setting. I began to hope that in living so close to volatile elements, I might become more sensitive to the invisible presences active in them. Living abroad for most of my adult life, the poetry of W.B. Yeats had provided imaginative continuity with the country of my birth. Through memorizing and pondering over the content of his poems I was often reminded that I too was one of a race that recognized its first unity in a mythology that married us to rock and hill. Sligo, where Yeats spent his childhood summers, was further north on the Connaught coastline. He and his friends at the turn of the twentieth century, had restored fairies to the landscape and presented readers and play-goers with a literature rooted in a legendary vision of history to counter the increasing materialism of the time. Here was a country of the mind in which I could orient myself and here I was at the source of it once more! Somebody had accused Yeats of having brought Irish weather into his verses thus altering the course of English literature forever.

Yeats' poetry conveys the urgency of nature spirits, their endless activity bred of the reciprocal relationship that operates between their realm and ours. Yeats and other Celtic renaissance poets revealed that it is a mutual devotion to the oversoul or folk spirit of Ireland that unites our hearts with the selfless activity of the spirits of air, water, fire, and earth. These beliefs fostered a spirit of nationhood as opposed to nationalism, that was more politically based. Just as the existence of spirit is the fountain of the manifold activities of the body so also is a love of nation spiritual in essence.

> *The mysterious element of beauty, of a peculiar beauty, exists in every nation and is the root cause of the love felt for it by the citizens.*
>
> From AE

A devotion to the feminine deity of the land through whom hope, protection, strength and harmony would issue, had characterized poetry in Irish literature in the eighteenth and nineteenth centuries. Yeats was writing out of this tradition when he gave us his splendid, even-prayerful tribute to the one he named Cathleen the daughter of Houlihan.

The old brown thorn trees break in two high over Cummen Strand,
Under a bitter, black wind that blows from the left hand;
Our courage breaks like an old tree in a black wind and dies
But we have hidden in our hearts a flame out of the eyes
Of Cathleen, the daughter of Houlihan.

The Call of Friendship

I was called away from the window by a light knock on my bedroom door. Frieda, the owner of the estate had come to welcome me. I had been struck by the warmth of Frieda's response when I had telephoned some weeks earlier to inquire about accommodation. The mellifluous tones of her voice were now matched by her gentle presence and striking beauty which was of the "black Irish" type. I had a sense of being restored to the company of a long lost sister and sensed a similar recognition in her. After we had discussed the practical details of my stay, I asked her to tell me the history of the house.

Frieda responded, "The estate was owned since the seventeenth century by a family called Purdon who distinguished themselves during the famine by their concern for the well-being of their tenants, making every effort to feed and clothe them. Those who survived the horrors of the time erected a plaque as an expression of gratitude to their landlord. This was most unusual. The title for the 300-acre property passed out of that family in 1901 and my husband and I acquired it in 1989 when it had fallen into a very dilapidated condition. We gradually managed to restore the property, preserving the original structure and character."

She continued animatedly, "We are, after all at the heart of Ireland here. This area was the focus of national attention at the close of the first millennium when Brian Boru, (whose seat of power, *Kincora*, was down the road) succeeded in vanquishing the Viking invaders. Ronald Reagan and others claim ancestry with the warrior king Brian."

Frieda continued: "The Irish name *Ti na Ranna*, means *house of the point*. I would like to establish a peaceful haven here for people seeking respite from the stress of modern life and provide a wide range of therapies for them."

"In the natural beauty of these surroundings people can experience the benefit of a healing current which is available twenty-four hours a day. I have lived for the past year in King View Farm, another such centre close to the city of Toronto in Canada. In that community I noticed that each member consciously serves the good of the whole which in turn reflects the talent and effort of each individual. This environment is ideal for anyone seeking refuge and renewal. I saw that when we pay attention to the needs of others our own needs are automatically served. *How these Christians love one another* was a phrase that sometimes entered my mind while I lived there, because love is always the source of our authenticity, our interest and our understanding of one another."

I find that I learn to know people by what I myself say in their company. It is my practice to orient myself in new situations by holding the question: "What is seeking to come forth here and how can I serve...?" Every angel of manifestation needs human minds and hearts and limbs to inspire and set into action. In adopting this approach I have been able to establish homes for myself in several places to which I have no material claim, but where the rightness of my spiritual bond with the people and place assures me a constant welcome.

"It is as though I have known you for a long time..." Frieda spoke after a long pause.

"I hope we will be good friends," I said sincerely.

A male friend of mine once wisely observed that when two women meet for the first time they exchange chapter and verse of interests and attitudes and cover more ground than the opposite gender would in years of acquaintance! Thus it was with us. As soon as my companion became aware of my familiarity with contemporary healing modalities she encouraged me to begin giving therapy sessions on the morrow. In this way I could join with the other therapists in serving a common purpose in an entirely practical way. It would also afford me the opportunity of meeting Irish people from every walk of life. "You will still have lots of time to write! I will also show you some walking trails. Let us meet at eight a.m., one or two mornings a week," she called over her shoulder as she left.

Christopher Bamford pointed out in a fine essay on the subject, that walking and friendship are inextricably linked. He writes that friends walk together *united in contemplation of the reality they aspire to...*

Aristotle noted that the wish for friendship develops rapidly but friendship does not. Friendships were based in either pleasure, utility or goodness, he thought. The latter was the most lasting because to wish for a friend's good for its own sake was the truest mark of friendship.

My most enduring friendships have survived misunderstandings, incompatibility of viewpoint, geographical distance, romantic attachment, disappointment as though to convince me and the other of the unassailable unity of our bond. Every call for forgiveness, every opportunity for growth, every pain of betrayal has been felt only in the context of friendship soured. Ralph Waldo Emerson had this vision of friendship.

> *Let it be an alliance of two large formidable natures, mutually beheld, mutually feared, before they recognize the deep identity which beneath these disparities unites them.*

In the introduction to one of his books, Irish writer James Stephens mentions a conversation he had with George Russell known to most people as AE.

> *"When you come to my age" said AE "If you can claim that you have had six friends in your life, you will be a luckier man than any man has a right to be."*
> *"I am one of your six," James boasted.*
> *"You are one of my four," he replied severely; and something like desolation fell on him for half a minute."*

AE was at the time easily the most popular man in Ireland!

Friendship arises out of a predisposition towards another person that can often be intuited at first meeting. A memory has been imprinted on the heart further back than we can remember. There is a recognition which cannot consciously be accounted for and sometimes even a feeling of awe, which causes a shyness to descend. It's as though a mystery lies ready to unfold in subsequent interaction.

Jesus, at the end of his ministry referred to his disciples as *friends*, thus introducing an ideal of friendship that is inclusive of intimacy with Him. All friendship will be tested by human shortcomings, but if we make brotherhood and sisterhood a constant recurring motif in our lives we will come close to leading a heavenly life on earth. I experience the vastness of my spiritual kin as I move from place to place. One of my sons reached a similar realization when he took to the road with the *Grateful Dead* in the early nineties, excitedly exclaiming to me one day. "Mom there isn't a town in the United States where I'm not welcome!"

Rudolf Steiner, writing at the turn of the last century, predicted that in the future every encounter between one human being and another would be sacramental in nature.

If we form an image of another person which is planted in our soul as a treasure, we carry part of him or her in our soul just as we carry something of our physical brother in our blood. Instead of merely blood relationships, spiritual relationships should form the basis of social life in this concrete way.

From Rudolf Steiner, The Challenge of the Times

Steiner also recommended that we awaken spirit in one another, a point that his contemporaries, W.B.Yeats and AE also stressed. The latter regarded the artist as spirit awakener supreme, believing that the artists were the true architects of a nation, shaping the collective consciousness out of their own imaginations. Native Americans proclaim the most eloquent amongst themselves *waker uppers*. James Joyce chose to fulfill a similar purpose when he undertook his monumental language alert calling it *Finnegans Wake*.

Inspired literature can serve to prepare our minds for the awakening that can most effectively come about through direct interaction with one another. Now in the twenty first century I believe we are called to this practice more than ever in the face of growing alienation, virtual reality, distrust, confusion and fear. We must value more than ever the life giving and soul strengthening nature of human relations. Self-absorption is a phase that most people, on a path of self-development, pass through. It is not the ultimate destination for anybody. Beyond that phase is the realization that in order to know oneself one must look out into the world and find one's deepest self reflected back in the events and people one encounters. The poet Novalis spoke from personal experience when he said, *The heart is the key to life and to the world. If our life is as precarious as it is, it is so in order that we should love and need one another.*

Spiritual Science, the path of esoteric schooling initiated by Rudolf Steiner, reveals how the hereditary forces that sustain the physical heart during childhood, begin to wither around the time of puberty. At the same time etheric forces strengthen to accommodate a more conscious life of feeling. An etheric or *phantom* heart hovers over the chest of every individual, clairvoyantly visible to a seer such as Dr. Steiner was. He observed it blossoming into a twelve-petalled flower as love for one's fellow man developed. As warmth of feeling flows between people the blood quickens in a health giving way, and love circulates throughout the universe as blood circulates in the human body. Rudolf Steiner's morning offering keeps me mindful of this reality.

> *In purest outpoured light*
> *Shimmers the godhead of the world*
> *In purest love towards all that lives*
> *Shimmers the godhead of my soul*
> *I rest within the godhead of the world*
> *There shall I find myself*
> *Within the godhead of the world.*

In this prayer is articulated the very essence of a sense of place. I only experience myself as truly at home in a place when I have established my purpose in being there, when I am attuned to the landscape, inhabitants and history of the area and when my individual aspirations can contribute to the collective well-being.

This demands adaptation to the subtle nuances of tradition and behavior that changing mores exacts. I knew that the content of my book would emerge from the ethos of this particular place and time as it impinged on my heart and mind. In this enterprise I would be led backwards, forwards and inwards like the movement of the threefold Celtic spiral, a metaphor for life itself.

I must be talking to my friends (W.B. Yeats)

Conversation is the lifeblood of communication, an artform that has fascinated me since childhood. As a little girl I developed very long ears, straining to catch the content of muffled adult talk behind closed doors. A protective silence hung around the affairs of the grown-up world which was considered too profane for innocent ears. "Curiosity killed the cat!" was the invariable response no matter how much the air was charged with the dynamic of some current happening. "What are they talking about?"— my sisters and I wondered. Instinctively I turned to books for the answers to questions I was not yet capable of formulating. Television had not yet been introduced in Ireland and I remained immersed in the kingdom of childhood while the soap operas of adult life unfolded around me and without my participation. I unconsciously adopted Rilke's outlook:

> *Be patient towards all that lies unsolved in your heart and try to live the questions themselves.*
> *Do not seek the answers that cannot be given you because you would not be able to live them. And the point is to live everything. Live the questions now. Perhaps you will gradually without noticing live along some distant day into the answers.*

The living into the answers will be ongoing for as long as I draw mortal breath. Many clues to the mystery have fallen from the lips of good talkers. I was eighteen when I met my first inspired talker. He was courting a younger sister, the beauty of our family. They married in due course although he was considerably older than she. His name was Tom Naughton and he had appeared in our small town in county Galway to salvage a business that was on the verge of ruin. He resembled the late John F. Kennedy who was a great hero of the Irish people. My sister was pregnant with their third child, when Tom lost his life in a car accident. His death left a void in the lives of hundreds of people— his absence is acutely felt even to this day.

He left many with an enhanced understanding of the meaning of friendship. His enduring support of friends in need, his gestures of practical assistance, depleted his own financial resources. People were the central focus of his life. He could divine and appreciate the unique individuality of the people who would gather around him, as round a hearth, often in the small hours of the morning. He was at his most insightful late at night, intent on bringing out the best in everyone, chiding and praising, holding up mirrors in the hilarious vignettes he performed extemporaneously. Years later I spent many happy hours in the company of the Irish actress Siobhán MacKenna, who spread a similar mantle of enchantment over any gathering, so that everyone could say afterwards, "Now I am more myself!" Time was away and somewhere else in the company of Tom or Siobhán who both taught me to be a good listener.

"What is a good listener?" James Stephens asked on the radio once and gave the following answer himself.

> *"A good listener is one who likes the person who is talking. This listening with affection is creative listening. No person, however gifted is talking at his best unless he likes the people he is talking to and knows that they like him, then he is inspired almost as a poet is."*

Stephens, who lived into the fifties of our era, could boast some of the greatest talkers Ireland has ever known as his contemporaries. They cultivated their art in the salons of the day which in the sixties, were superseded by such pubs in Dublin as the Bailey and McDaids.

The tradition of home salon was still upheld by a few in the Ireland of my time. I was invited to Arland Usher's Friday nights whenever I was in Dublin and thereby acquired a sense of the purpose and character of such gatherings. Arland, in earlier years, had himself enjoyed the soirees of A.E. and Yeats. He rarely spoke at his own gatherings but sat chainsmoking in a corner with a look of glee on his face. He was known in Dublinese to be *a great man for the women* but he was seen to be resting from his escapades on these occasions. His silent focus seemed to fuel discussion in the assembled company of voluble writers and actors he attracted. But I cannot remember encountering any talker there or elsewhere with the remarkable quality James Stephens attributed to his friend Stephen McKenna to whom famous writers such as Yeats, AE, Joyce had to accede in conversation.

> *"But his remarkable and never absent great quality was that he not only made his listeners listen, he made his listeners talk. When you were with McKenna you discovered that you were talking just as much as he was. For the first time in your life perhaps, you found that you were also a philosopher, a wit, a lover of the moon, and an intimate of Eve and of the dragon, the donkey and the duck."*

Treasa O'Driscoll

Ireland has often been characterized as a nation of talkers and all the best talk can be traced in its origins to the Irish language termed by Synge, *the language of a race that has tired the sun with talking...*

The English language of Synge's plays, carries the character of the Irish tongue, so full of hyperbole, cajolery, lamentations, euphemism, allusion, endearment, blessing and tirade. The people who shaped the language owed nothing to book learning but regarded an original turn of phrase as an expression of individuality to be cultivated and respected. Language to them was the fruit of the deeds and sufferings of life, which rendered one person distinct from another. How you spoke and what you said was more important than how you looked or what you owned. Healthy speech was seen to give rise to physical health and to maintain the spiritual well-being of the speaker. Synge's characters were closely modeled on people who surrounded him on the Aran Islands, the people he met walking the roads of Ireland. He described their talk as follows:

> *A fashion of speech which was not conned from books, the wild exuberant speech of isolated people. People who are as timid in action as they are bold in talk; being bold indeed in the only thing they have practice of.*

Robin Flower was a scholar who immortalized the Gaelic speech and ways of the Blasket Islands, off the southwest coast of Ireland. Peig Sayers was one of its most famous inhabitants living there in rhythmic harmony with the elements. Although illiterate she had a great gift of articulation. He came upon her cursing one day.

> *"The people of the island have a fine gift of cursing," I said.*
> *"We have," she answered, "but there is no sin in it. If the curse came from the heart, it would be a sin. But it is from the lips they*

come, and we use them only to give force to our speech, and they are a great relief to the heart."

"Well," I said, "I make little of them, for if the blessings come from the heart I don't care where the curses come from."

The Loss of Language

More tragic than the disruption caused in the history of the Irish people by famine, is the social disintegration that arose and that continues to prevail since the native language was virtually eliminated as a mother tongue. A concerted campaign was successfully conducted in the seventeenth and eighteenth centuries to cause people to abandon Irish in all but the few peripheral pockets where it is still spoken today. Complex and cruel in its implementation, it demanded that parents punish their children as a means of censor. The parents themselves were already enslaved and weakened in spirit by poverty and hunger. Its repercussions on the national psyche can still be felt. The shift from Irish to English and the cultural fragmentation that resulted is one of the hidden causes of mass emigration from the country. Economic deprivation can be overcome in one generation but the loss of the natural expression of a collective psyche can never be overcome.

I see the backlash in evidence in Ireland's metamorphosis into a consumer society. Greed and self-interest predominate in the absence of a common cultural ideal. When people lose spiritual identity they seek its substitute in material things.

Irish life is like a plant which has been cut back to the roots, but which cannot grow again because it is being continually trampled on, Sean de Freine states in his seminal book, *The Great Silence*.

AE, among others, sowed the seeds of Ireland's spiritual renewal which remain yet to be harvested.

> ...We are less children of this clime
> Than of some nation yet unborn
> Or empire in the womb of time
> We hold the Ireland in the heart
>
> More than the land our eyes have seen
> And love the goal for which we start
> More than the thought of what has been...
>
> *From AE, In Defence of Some Irishmen
> Not Followers of Tradition*

AE was disheartened because, for 700 years, generations had fought for the liberation of the Irish folk soul, beautiful Caitlín Ní Uallacháin. And when they set her free, Lady Gregory remarked, that she walked out, like a fierce vituperative old hag.

> *Alas it is the curse of our public life that men too often choose to maintain causes rather than their own human worth and they think their country is served thereby as if any cause was higher than the character of human life in it.*
>
> *From AE,* The Homestead, *1912*

Ireland has, in the intervening years paid the price for materialism in the obliteration of her soul and her countryside, but I believe it is still possible in our day of spiritual awakening to raise the soul of Ireland nearer to the ideals held so courageously by our visionary writers. It will be accomplished now by individual people taking their own spiritual development in hand and engaging in collective endeavour as free self- actualized human beings.

Frieda and I talked of these and other matters as we took our first walk through the unspoiled landscape of County Clare, conversing in the Irish language which was so dear to both our hearts. I struggled to keep pace with her, being unused to such early morning exertion. It was an occasion of *deja vu* as we climbed uphill. I could vividly recall similar walks and animated exchanges in Irish during my teenage years as a boarder in a convent in County Mayo which was set like Tinarana on the shores of a lake, Lough Mask. Half of my classmates were from Connemara and Irish was their first language. Some of them were descendants of the Aran Islanders who had inspired the plays of John Millington Synge. They spoke in musical tones, with the clear intonation, the attention to vowels and the richness of expression that I have ever since associated with the Irish language.

As we rounded the hill we both fell silent, a stillness seemed to descend as the light became golden in a turquoise haze. Trees and landscape appeared embossed in this moment of unearthly radiance. We looked at one another, transfigured in a tableau that is etched in my memory. I felt touched by divine grace and filled with cheerful confidence of all that was to come. The artist's eye was open to the awesome beauty of the scene. *"I wish I had paint and canvas with me now,"* Frieda murmured. We began to talk about the connection between memory and feeling.

"We have as it were, two memories, one that recalls facts, details, dates, chapter and verse and which can also go blank, a memory that can be stored in a computer. This memory serves physical life predominately and we need it to function effectively in the world. The other memory, the hidden aspect of memory arises when love and intuition are at work." I ventured. Looking at her watch Frieda remarked: "I am remembering that it is time for me to go to work!"

When I returned to my room I looked up a reference Professor Lorna Reynolds (who had been my husband's

Treasa O'Driscoll

closest friend), had made to Martin Heidegger's book, *What is Called Thinking*.

Her gloss is as follows: *memory* he wrote, *initially did not at all mean the power to recall... originally memory means as much as devotion: a constant concentrated abiding with something, and it involves not only the power of recall, but also the power of unrelinquishing and unrelenting retention.*

Professor Reynolds adds that it is only when the heart thinks, giving thanks in thought that poetry arises and gives birth to philosophy.

I resolved to remember my life and relationships in the spirit of this statement and with all the devotion implied by Christian Morgenstern in the following lines:

...With thankfulness resounds all life divine
Resounds from beings one and manifold
In giving thanks all beings intertwine.

> *One charge alone we give to youth*
> *Against the sceptered myth to hold*
> *The golden heresy of truth.*
> *A.E.*

Three

HERESIES OF TRUTH

Spring was at hand. Country roads became more enticing, sap rising and circulating in every living thing. Hedges and trees were coming back to themselves, awakening from the anonymity of winter sleep. Skies appeared more clement, roadside streams and trickling waterfalls more musical, the swell of birdsong more assured. Change was in the air sweeping me up in its current...

Trunks bearing the totality of my earthly possessions arrived from Canada. I was eager to surround myself with cherished books and paintings once again. By fortunate synchronicity the Tinarana gate lodge became available to rent and within days I was ensconced in the modest though modernized two-roomed dwelling. In-built bookshelves were soon swelling, a sturdy desk and chair rested between heater and fireplace and the freshly painted walls afforded ample gallery space. I hung the prized works of Canadian painter friends between the windows so I could watch slanting sunlight enhance the subtle and vibrant colors. Never in all my wanderings had I found a more perfect setting for these paintings nor felt so well surrounded by them. Cottage windows presented seasonal splendors of budding foliage, gnarled tree trunks, a blaze of yellow furze that would last several months and the highs and lows of bushes. There was pleasure without end in the drama of skies against which distant blue and purple hills presided majestically over acres of woodland and lake. The enchantment deepened when I stepped outside. Imposing oaks, beeches and sycamores, a Spanish chestnut shading my doorway, were protective and reassuring in their sheltering presence. I had been loathe to abandon the luxury of the big house and the illusions of grandeur I could indulge in there but I was, I reminded myself, still within pleasant tree-lined walk of it. More peripheral to me now would be the comings and goings of guests and the idle chat I so enjoyed. The time had come for me to forego all distraction if I was to meet my deadline, feel the earth beneath my feet and face for the first time in my life the challenge of living alone. As if to affirm the rightness of the move, a letter arrived from Jay Ramsay, a favorite contemporary poet, within hours of my settling in.

Included was a poem entitled *For Treasa*. It recalled the occasion, a few months before, of our stay in an establishment known as An Culturlann, in rooms high up on the fourth floor. There we had ranged in rambling talk late into the night. Jay penned these lines:

In Belgrave Square, Monkstown, Co Dublin
Where we were soon to give a reading in
a millionaire's house
Five hundred yards down the traffic torn road...

The irony of our situation had not been lost on us... two impecunious artists helping wealthy people to raise money for a worthy cause. Jay's compassionate interest in my circumstances brought me close to tears and I could confess to him how difficult it was for me to adapt to an impoverished way of life. He urged me to embrace whatever reality I was faced with, explaining that acceptance would lead me into authenticity. My transference now from mansion to mews was a symptom of that new found practicality. It was encouraging for me therefore to note the uncanny accuracy and timeliness of the lines Jay addressed to me:

how are you going to descend?

And the temptation is to ignore it
When the sun comes out again
To let the universe bail us out
But isn't that the beginning of sadness?
Not to stand in our own two feet
and in what we speak
But to embody it and bear the world
As the time demands, if we are to be
what we dream.

Because as far as we reach upwards
we have to come down
To grasp the nettle of matter beneath,
Powerless as we are beside the rain
and falling leaves

And when we can let go to them; peace,
In the deep solace of quiet they seek....

In fact the universe *had* bailed us out on that occasion, our good deed rewarded a hundred-fold. We had both been offered book contracts the morning after the reading, one of the most remarkable examples of divine providence I have ever witnessed!

Now and Then
>A wall of forest looms above
>and sweetly the blackbird sings;
>All the birds make melody
>over me and my books and things.
>
>There sings to me the cuckoo
>from bush citadels in grey hood,
>God's doom! May the Lord protect me
>Writing well, under the great wood.

This rhapsodic gloss, curiously fitting for me now, was inscribed by a monk on the margin of a ninth century manuscript. My fondness for the old mysteries could, I thought, be fruitfully sustained in the proximity of a grove of oak trees, named in Irish *doire*, root word for *druid*, he who plied his priestly craft underneath their shade. The continuity of the druidic calling was later vested in the filí [poets]—guardians of oral tradition who through their learning and imagination could honor and reveal the secrets of creation.

When I had first surveyed the mere 500 sq. ft. of cottage floor I remarked to the young man who had unlocked the door for me: "You couldn't swing a cat in here!"

"Well," he said somewhat scornfully, "it ought to be big enough for you. My relations managed to raise a family of ten here years ago."

No more complaints from me!

Stepping inside, I imagined how it might once have been—a one-roomed cottage, family all huddled around an open hearth, a hanging black kettle boiling over a turf fire, the smoky atmosphere permeated by the smell of burning peat, the glow of an oil lamp penetrating the darkness, bedding made of straw and horsehair dimly perceptible in a corner. Perhaps this cottage stood on the foundations of a cabin that might have fallen into ruin during the famine? I had recently come across accounts written in trembling hand by concerned visitors to Ireland in the early eighteen hundreds. Words often failed them in the depiction of the abject poverty of families living in hovels containing no furniture at all. One million people had perished between 1845-50, their emaciated bodies withered or swollen with disease. In the towns the straggling columns of haunted wretches trooping to already overcrowded poorhouses, were a heart-wrenching sight. Lying on the streets were dying children, orphaned and alone, their empty expressions giving hunger and despair a face. The breathtaking beauty of the Clare landscape held a memory of suffering, the clay of skeletal corpses had mingled with the brown earth and nourished its verdure. The untimely surrender of bodies to mass graves on sloping hillsides released curses and blessings that still affect the living.

Reading the traveler's accounts of famine in Ireland, I was reminded of a conversation that I had with an elderly friend whose grandparents had lived through the famine. As we discussed the tragedy of starvation Richard said with characteristic insight, "Suffering has different meanings for people. Christianity has rooted itself deeply in the Irish psyche. The sacrifice of Christ Jesus, his prolonged passion has inspired in us an *art of suffering*. Perhaps it is not so prevalent in the Ireland of today but it certainly was, up to thirty years ago."

"What you say reminds me of something Simone Weil has written," I countered, reaching for a book from its shelf. She makes a distinction between suffering and affliction. Suffering she argues has a psychological connotation which can sometimes be perversely indulged in, people have a tendency to view themselves as victims because of the attention it attracts. However, she describes affliction as being more endemic to a Christian approach. *It is not a psychological state; it is a mechanical brutality of circumstances.* And although affliction is something imposed, often to the horror and revulsion of the victim, Simone Weil states that this is the very thing one must consent to, by virtue of supernatural love. Leafing through the book I found her definition of love which I had underlined—*the necessary force of nature in its brute ongoing impulse of destruction leading to growth, leading to death...* I read, closing the book.

Richard sat for a moment in contemplative silence then quietly remarked, "I always sense that our famine ancestors were predisposed to make that consent and that our task is to forgive and live our lives all the more fully and freely because of their sacrifice."

Later I picked up the famine book again *(A Seat Behind the Coachman)* to resume a reading of the accounts of an English traveler in Ireland in 1834.

> *The lower orders of the Irish have much feeling for each other. It is a rare thing to hear an angry or contemptuous expression addressed to anyone who is poor; commiseration of the destitute condition of others is largely mingled in their complaints of their own poverty, and it is a fact that they are most exemplary in the care which they take of their destitute relatives and in the sacrifices which they willingly make for them.*

Although this was written more than one hundred years before I was born, this mood of soul was prevalent in the people who surrounded me in childhood. Generosity was valued as the virtue that covered a multitude of sins. There was ample opportunity for giving to the poor. *Tinkers*—those descendants of tenants evicted during the famine, who never again succeeded in settling and to this day, live in caravans along Irish roads, were ever at our door and we knew them each by name. In my town they were all called Ward, the English version of *bard*, the bards being the first Irish itinerants who sang for their suppers. Instead of songs the tinkers of my day offered prayers. They would need to be permanently on their knees to offer up all the supplications they rashly promised on the receipt of pennies or scraps of food!

Habits of prayer were inculcated in me from an early age, the legacy of generations for whom every act was accompanied by the remembrance of God, getting up, kindling the fire, sitting down to eat, working, going to bed. There were of course prayers for special occasions and always *aspirations*—the constant remembrance of the souls in purgatory. One of my favorite translations from the Irish covers all eventualities.

May not the grass that grows, nor the sand on the shore, nor the dew on the pasture be more plentiful than the blessings of the King of Grace on every soul that was, that is, that will be.

For many years of my life I lost this mindfulness of Divine presence but esoteric studies led me back to its simple effectiveness again. Mother Meera, an Indian avatar who makes her home in Europe, demonstrates through word and deed how simplicity can restore us to the Light. Her way is consistent with ancient Irish practice: *Offering everything, pure and impure, is the best and quickest way to develop spiritually. If you offer everything to the Divine, the Divine will accept and change it, even the worst things. It is not what you offer but THAT you offer, which is important. Offer everything, and you will acquire the habit of thinking always about God. THAT will change you.* This is what I was able to teach my daughter and sons in later life.

Transcending Tradition

Robert Frost makes reference to *that something there is that does not love a wall* in us. I suffered as a child the discomfort of interminable church ceremonies, the rigmarole of sermons, and moribund adherence to Latin rituals when I longed to be out in the fresh air playing with my friends. Reading books upside down at age five, I was indicating an inborn need to explore a world beyond the bounds of inherited belief. I was not predisposed to taking truth on somebody else's authority or to identifying with un-examined assumptions.

The religious instruction I received as a child included a lamentation about the original sin of Adam and Eve to which we are heirs. Their mistake, I understood, was to have partaken of the Tree of Knowledge when God had provided them with the Tree of Life which was all He intended for them at that time. Ironically this error, instead of being righted, was assiduously upheld in the classrooms of my childhood where dogma took precedence over experience. Children of my generation were induced—on pain of that humiliation anathema to a child—to learn by rote, statements of theological import beyond the grasp of our innocent minds. Questions and answers spun out of the abstractions of theologians could and often did effectively subdue any spirit of enquiry. We were led to believe that only a card-carrying Catholic would be recognized by St. Peter at the gates of Heaven, the destination for which life on earth was but mere preparation. The promise of such ultimate distinction went a long way in the acceptance of doctrine however daft some of it was. I subscribed to some fanciful beliefs which have since been retracted. Gone for instance is the notion of limbo, that no-mans-land to which the souls of babies who died in the womb or before baptism were condemned, *never to see the face of God for all eternity*. Gullible parents suffered the intense agony of this belief to compound their loss. I also used to have vivid imaginations of myself burning in hell until I awoke to the realization that I would not after all have a body at that point, for the literal flames to lick!

Continuity Through Change

The coming of Christianity to Ireland and the British Isles is shrouded in mystery. In the sixth century the Welsh bard Taliesin declared:

> *Christ the Word from the beginning was, from the beginning our Teacher, and we never lost His teaching. Christianity was in Asia a new thing but there was never a time when the druids of Britain held not its doctrines.*

Another writer named Gildas claimed in the same century:
> *These islands received the beams of light.... in the latter part of the reign of Tiberius Caesar, in whose time this religion was propagated...without impediment or death.*

History dates the reign of this King circa 37 A.D. Scholars maintain that early Christianity was established in parts of Britain, not accessible to the Romans. Legend provides a clue to its arrival in England by grace of Joseph of

Arimethea, the bearer of the precious chalice of the Holy Grail. He and twelve companions built a round church of clay and wattles in Glastonbury. Ireland's special status was marked even earlier, its ground hallowed. It is said that this piece of earth represents a portion of Paradise which separated out before it could be contaminated by the temptation of Lucifer.

Mythological stories and the oral tradition carry evidence of an ancient state of consciousness that experienced itself as being *in* and *of* nature, with no duality of subjective - objective. Consequently the whole elemental world was permeated with meaning, suffusing the world of the senses. This quality of perception continued in Ireland for centuries and informed early Christianity. The unity of all living forms was clairvoyantly known when the poet-seer of our first Irish ancestors, the Milesians, gave utterance to the following words, on first setting foot on Irish soil.

> I am an estuary into the sea
> I am a wave of the ocean
> I am the sound of the sea
> I am a powerful ox
> I am a hawk on a cliff
> I am a dewdrop in the sun...

To apprehend something was to directly experience it. In eastern epistemology this is known as *that I am*. This form of old clairvoyance, began to fade as intellect started to develop in the human race. We had to experience separation from the whole in order to observe, evaluate, invent and exploit. Form began to take precedence over content. Losing sight of our spiritual origins fear entered earthly life and its corollary, despair.

The ability to look through appearance and into the reality of things persisted in certain individuals and their way of describing events took the longer view into account and mankind's foundation in a spiritual world. Whoever wrote the following verse quoted by Alexander Carmichael in *Prayers and Blessings from the Gaelic*, was aware of the spiritual state of darkness within human souls that could only be alleviated through divine intervention.

> A time ere came the Son of God
> The earth was a bleak morass,
> Without star, without sun, without moon,
> Without body, without heart, without form.
> Illuminated plains, illuminated hills,
> Illuminated the great green sea
> Illuminated the whole globe together,
> When the Son of God came to earth...

The understanding of the cosmic as well as historical significance of Christ Jesus inspired the teaching of Irish saints and monks. We may glean from them, in the words of H.J. Massingham, *a gleam of the new philosophy of heaven and earth in interdependence and interaction, formulated by a culture in vital contact with the ancient nature worship*. The Celts were among the races who worshipped the sun. For them, the sun was the eye and raiment of the Divine. They regarded the sun as the highest principle of creation, which revealed itself to them in the mythic form of Lugh, god of light. The ancient Persians called this being Ahura Masda, to the Indians he was Deva; the Egyptians hailed him as Osiris; he was Apollo to the Greeks. In the old religions people designated themselves children of the sun. Some remnants of old Solstice rites survived in my native Galway at the turn of the twentieth century. Women still engaged in the traditional ceremonial walk around a symbolic sun fire, encircling it twelve times.

Midwinter festivals were celebrated in Egypt, Asia and Europe long before the birth of Christ. Druids in the Celtic regions conducted fire festivals to assert their confidence in the power of the sun. The dependence of all rhythmic life upon the sun appears at one time to have been directly experienced all over the world. Although the same reality applies today we no longer have conscious experience of the harmony of the sun's path reflected in our pulse, breathing and digestive process. We can only know *about* it. It is a matter of choice now whether we conduct our lives in keeping with cosmic rhythm or not. All disaster (*adrift from the stars*) and chaos arises from a lack of alignment with cosmic order. The whole spectrum of cause and effect can take literally ages to manifest.

The mythological homage to the Sun Being prefigured and prepared human consciousness for the coming of Christ. He exists eternally as harmonizing Sun Being within human consciousness stirring and illuminating the unredeemed regions of our subconscious where habit, resistance and addiction are harbored. The activity of transformation and renewal initiated when the Christ Light assumed human form, continues in every epoch. His incarnation was an act of divine intervention that changed the course of human life forever, a cosmic deed central to the Irish lore of my childhood.

Yeats tells the well-known story of King Concubhar and Buchrach, a druid. As they sat in discourse on the original Good Friday, Concubhar noticed *the unusual changes in creation and the eclipse of the sun and the moon at its full.* Buchrach informs him that *Jesus Christ, the Son of God is even now being crucified. The* version printed in my schoolbook (when I was a young girl) was entitled *The First Man Ever to*

Die for Christ. I remember how proud the nun who was my teacher seemed that an Irishman held that distinction! She read to us aloud about the King who had been told by his doctor to remain calm because of a *brain ball* which had lodged in his skull. When the druid relayed the events of Christ's final hours to the king he became so incensed that he rushed out of his castle and began to beat down bushes, his frenzy leading to the dislodgment of the *brain ball*, leading to his death.

Imbued with the Christ force that penetrates the natural and human worlds, and a heartfelt understanding of the Christian mystery, Irish monks brought a revival of culture as well as an informed spirituality to the monastic tradition they cultivated throughout Europe. Each epoch has had its own mystery schools where pupils have been initiated into higher levels of consciousness. I think the contemporary mystery wisdom of Ireland, once termed Hibernia, is something that we make up as we go along. Magic or mystery, in Irish *draiocht*, is said to be comprised of three elements - *ceo* [mist], *ceol* [music], and *seoltóireacht* [sailing], a combination of intrigue, rhythm and movement. The clue relating to music brings us back to a story about Fionn and the Fianna, mythological warriors, led by a seer.

> *Once as they rested on a chase, a debate arose among the Fianna-Finn as to what was the finest music in the world.*
>
> *'Tell us, chief,' one ventured, 'what do you think?'*
>
> *'The music of what happens' said the great Fionn, 'that is the finest music in the world!'*

We make entry into *the music of what happens* by way of presence, poetry and pilgrimage - the three elements at the core of the Celtic way which may be adapted to any time or place.

The Sun in You

The Christ reveals himself to me as an eternal exchange of love between persons. Just as wisdom permeates the natural world, love permeates our human world as the reality in which we live. Regardless of what form this love may take, romantic, platonic, sexual, familial, our commitment to the growth and flourishing of a planet of love requires that we develop the willingness to live unconditionally on the creative edge, calm in the face of uncertainty, doubt and apprehension, remaining consistently present to whatever arises. It requires our increased ability to respond—responsibility towards everyone and everything we encounter. Each life is an experiment in the individual expression of love in thought, feeling and action.

We are no longer as subject as we once were to the constraints of convention. We are learning to continue to love even when the circumstances make it uncomfortable for us to do so. The demand of the time is that we develop a discipline of love.

> *We develop psychological, physiological or neurological theories to explain its beginnings, but have no actual experience, no connection with its source. Love can only be known through loving and we are left completely to ourselves to find out what love may be.*
> From *Robert Sardello,* Love and the Soul

There is a passage in the Gospel of St. Matthew that seems particularly pertinent to our time. *And because deeds of violence against the heavenly law multiply, the love of the many will grow cold.* When we receive the media accounts of all the atrocities being perpetuated today it engenders hopelessness and a sense of powerlessness. When we think it is pointless to go on feeling, the power to love is dulled. I frequently cry if I watch the news on television and offer up my feelings of frustration to the Divine Mother calling to mind the image of Michelangelo's *Pieta*. The flow of tears helps to keep the heart always warm. Nobody has ready answers for the unprecedented happenings of this time and difficult as it may be for people who regard answers as being more important than questions, more and more people are learning to accustom themselves to not knowing. I find that when I entertain a question I soon begin to feel the steady beat of an answering response implicit in my environment. This in itself awakens love for one's own time and place.

The work of preparing human hearts for the task of Love was begun by the druids. Rudolf Steiner relates how the druid priest, at the Summer Solstice, stood in the centre of a circle of twelve stones - each stone representative of a petal of the lotus flower that hovers over every heart. He was anticipating the day when these flowers would fully unfold in the experience of every life, knowing that souls would radiate a field of love when hearts grew warm and loving.

John Davy, onetime editor of the London Observer, and master of Emerson College when I knew him, was an important teacher for me who spoke the language of the heart. He wrote before his untimely death in the early 1980's:

Just as the sun of nature shines on the whole earth so the time has come for a sun to shine from human hearts. This sun cannot be possessed by any one group or religion. It will illumine all religions that come from the past and celebrate the divinity in all humanity.

The raying of this inner sunshine will eventually make it impossible for us to affect indifference to the plight of others, fulfilling Rudolf Steiner's selfless prayer.

> As long as you feel pain
> which I am spared
> So is Christ's deed
> unrecognized in the world.
> For weak is still the spirit
> Who can only suffer in his
> own body.

The Heretical Edge

In the Irish language we say, *Tá mo chroí istigh ionat* – 'my heart is inside you' as a more precise and traditional way of saying *I love you*. When we give undivided attention to what surrounds us, be it nature, architecture, painting, music, literature or other people, we put our hearts inside everything and in that way come to intimate knowledge of things.

It was in the pursuit of this learning through love that the great monastic schools flourished in fifth, sixth, and seventh century Ireland. There the seven liberal arts were practiced while Europe was undergoing what has been termed, a dark age. When that phase came to an end, the saints and scholars took to the high seas and enlivened the courts of Europe with their learned discourse, finding pupils everywhere willing to devote themselves to the study of wisdom and scripture. Celtic spirituality endured, enlivened always by heresy and a healthy spirit of enquiry. The church today would do well to incorporate teachings that once threatened its composure but which may at last be assimilated into twenty first century consciousness. Christian mysticism which took shape in monastic solitude was once regarded as the highest form of spiritual life. Inspired mystics ever embraced unorthodox forms of spirituality and aroused the suspicions of the authorities, both Catholic and Protestant, leading to inquisition and persecution. Those whose lives and thoughts were most exemplary were often condemned while hypocrisy and mediocrity and literal mindedness flourished, as it always does, with the politically correct of every epoch.

The concern of inquisitors and their successors is more with the preservation of forms and rituals than with the spiritual enlightenment of the individual. The tragedy of the heretics was that their philosophy was somewhat ahead of their time - human consciousness being only now perhaps ripe enough to grasp the truth of medieval heresies. Heretics were denounced for asserting that union with the Divine is the goal of human life—implying this life and not only the life hereafter. Meister Eckhart, a universally significant teacher and a casualty of inquisition, cannot fail to appeal to modern seekers for the clarity and relevance of his sermons and treatises. I admire most of all his courage in the face of opposition and his claims for the spark of divinity inherent in each of us. He lived at what has been termed the dawn of the modern age, its conditions curiously prefiguring present times. It was a time of temporal and spiritual uncertainty, abnormal natural phenomena, earthquakes, severe winters, famine and disease. Dire external events and a failure in church guidance prompted people of the middle ages to seek essential truths of spirit through their own life experience.

Many people, of whom Eckhart was one, believed in the doctrine of the *Free Spirit* which proclaimed that the entire church as it was then constituted, was destined to pass away. In its place would emerge a new era in human spirituality based on the inner consciousness of God. Another common theme among heretics was their future hope that the churches of east and west would unite and the world become *a vast monastery populated by human beings with 'spiritual bodies' in unity with God.*

The natural tendency of the human mind to bolster itself with the rational, the familiar and the known, will always characterize upholders of organized religion. But the spark within the human spirit which fires the mystic experience transcends the constraints of time and space and invariably finds its place in poetry. It is to this stream that I am inherently drawn.

What we term Celtic Spirituality is a force of truth that maintained continuity through change. Evident at one time in the Egyptian Desert Fathers, it emerged later in Ireland, then moved through medieval Europe informing the consciousness of Erigena, Hildegard of Bingen, St Francis of Assisi, Eckhart, Tauler and others. It appeared in the mystic writings of Jacob Boehme, Goethe, Blake and in the writers of the Irish Literary Renaissance. It has surfaced for me in the work of contemporary poets too numerous to mention but referred to often in these pages. It became most accessible to me through the study of Rudolf Steiner's Spiritual Science which contains a contemporary synthesis of all the above and manifests as a significant world movement of renewal in many areas of life, social, educational, medical, agricultural and artistic.

The inspired writings of Yeats and AE were my bridge between Irish tradition and esoteric teachings. Many years ago I memorized *Ribh Considers Christian Love Insufficient* by Yeats. I later encountered corresponding concepts in the writings of Eckhart.

> *For everything the understanding can grasp, and everything desire demands is not God. Where understanding and desire have an end, there it is dark,*

there does God shine... The more the soul is empty of all things which are not God, the more purely she receives God, the more she is in God, and the more she becomes one with God.

Centuries later, W.B. Yeats wrote:

...Then my delivered soul herself shall learn
A darker knowledge and in hatred turn
From every thought of God mankind has had.
Thought is a garment and the soul's a bride
That cannot in that trash and tinsel hide:
Hatred of God may bring the soul to God...

I recite the last line of this verse as though it were written: *Hatred of '**God**', may bring the soul to God.* In fact my soul journey and that of many people I know is perfectly encapsulated here by a great poet whose legacy became interwoven with the events of my own life.

Treasa O'Driscoll

> *"Ireland is the best country to live out of."*
> George Birmingham

Four

TO GO FORTH SINGING

My cultural identity with the *splendors of the Gael* is as strong as ever today despite my more than half a life time spent living abroad. I have set down sporadic roots in eastern and western Canada and in the southern United States, adapting as needed to the peculiar ethos of each new environment. Like myself, most of my North American friends were born on a different continent. I have come to view each person as a living culture, of which nationality is an aspect, engaged in vital dialogue with the people, circumstances and surroundings of the moment. My way of being has been influenced by the expansive generosity of Americans, the tolerance and compassion so marked in Canadian people, the cultivated estheticism of French people and the dedicated work ethic of Germans. The Irish were traditionally a source of amusement to Americans, viewed as fighting, praying or drinking when not engaged in dancing jigs or seeing leprechauns. Many people are predisposed to being charmed by us, consequently mere Irishness can almost constitute a profession. We can be most completely ourselves it seems when not limited by the preconceptions of those who know us well.

The urge to escape the homogeneity of my homeland lent distant shores distinct allure for me. Not surprisingly I fell in love with a Newfoundlander. More Irish than the Irish themselves in ways, he was yet distinctly foreign with none of the predictable traits I could identify in my compatriots. Canada became my country of adoption when I married him and the country in which I still feel most at home. Yet songs and stories are my permanent mark of Irishness for those who know me. Only in three of my children has the metamorphosis to Irish-Canadian been complete. My eldest son has restored himself to the Clare origins of his ancestors as though the continuum between my grandfather's life and his had never been interrupted, like an unbroken melody.

A priest of my acquaintance spent many years in Africa, inspired by the vitality of the tradition he encountered there. He related how in a particular tribe, the beginning of a person's life is traced back to a thought in the mother's mind, to the moment in which she recognizes the prospective father. As she sits underneath a tree full of the momentum of possibility, she begins to hear the song of the unborn child. She teaches the song to her man and together they intone, calling the incarnating soul towards them in their lovemaking. During the pregnancy all the villagers learn the song of the child. Everyone sings it during the birth of this new member of their community. The

Treasa O'Driscoll

song will accompany every life event and will swell in celebration at a marriage ceremony which holds the promise of more songs. At the end of life this song will deepen into a keening, for its melody can effect joy and sorrow and all the changing moods of life.

My friend remarked after telling this story to a group of us: "By infusing the music into every cell of your body, the divine Mother called you into earthly incarnation and her song will keep you in her fold throughout your life and draw you into Her eternal embrace when you cross death's threshold."

"What a comfort that practice must be for the people of that place," I said.

"The song of life is in everybody. Listen to that song in your own heart. Allow it to guide you." He replied.

Entering into the spirit of his words I thought and later said, "Truths which are eternally enshrined in powerful storytelling traditions around the world are transmitted with equal force in our Western poetic tradition. D.H. Lawrence has given us a poem entitled *Deeper than Love* which identifies a profound guiding source within each one of us:

> O love is a deep thing
> but there are deeper things
> than love….

Lawrence knew that truth is what nourishes love. I hear my own song echoing back to me in these verses just as the African would hear his in an encounter with a member of his tribe. I began to recite:

> …Oh long before love is possible
> passion has roused in the soul
> the primordial passion of truth
> is awake, the passion for life,

and the passion to be aware of life,
For truth, oldest mystery of the consciousness,
is passionate awareness of life...

Poems and stories like the foregoing help us to remember our spiritual origins. The melody of truth is sustained in my heart by a growing capacity to hear it resonate in the hearts of people I meet as I pursue the path of bardic performer and workshop leader. Sometimes its echo is faint, at other times clear. Every speaking voice is distinct and resonant with the innate melody of the speaker. A poet hears his own song more acutely than most and gives it an expression to which all can respond. Yeats' song called him to *Innisfree*, a lush island off the coast of Sligo where he spent his childhood summers.

...I will arise and go now, for always
night and day
I hear lake water lapping with
low sounds by the shore;
While I stand on the roadway,
or on the pavements grey,
I hear it in the deep heart's core.

Even when walking the pavements of the bustling city of London through the hum of traffic, Yeats could discern the gentle sounds of lapping waters murmuring his name and calling him home.

Bardic Calling

A similar yearning drew me into the well established stream of bardic tradition. The brilliant, exciting and dynamic man I fell in love with and married was a distinguished professor in the field of Irish Studies. He generously facilitated my interests and regularly invited me to share my songs and stories with his students who were eager to hear sounds in the Irish vernacular. The extraordinary richness of our native language is evident in every page of my well thumbed *Dineen's Irish Dictionary*. The hilarious disparity in the meanings of certain words is demonstrated in the following example:

(a) a rare disease in sheep, or
(b) a loud sound made in an empty house by an unauthorized person.

I like to claim the lineage of *reacaire*. Dineen defines the term as: "an auctioneer, a seller, a reciter, a story teller, a gossiper, a poet's repetitor, a ranting female." The reacaire ranked close to that of original "god sybil" from which the word "gossiper" emerged.

The surname O'Driscoll, supports the description of storyteller and reciter. O'Drisceoil, not only includes the word *ceol* [music], it is a name derived in old Irish from *Uidersceol* [between stories] and *Idir scéil* [an intermediary]. Every name has its own vibration and, when assumed and not inherited, a name can often sit uneasily with a person's true nature. In my case this surname called forth an innate talent, as did the whole way of life I entered into with my marriage and departure from Ireland. Our home in Toronto became a kind of unofficial Irish embassy, a first port-of-call for Irish scholars, poets, musicians and artists, a centre of hospitality where ideas were freely shared and animated discussion continued late into the night. We provided what little we had, pouring gallons of tea and whiskey for some of the finest talkers in the world. It was a phase of my apprenticeship when I acquired the skills of a good listener which includes the ability to sense what will or will not hold the attention of an audience.

The reciter who accompanied the bard in earlier centuries, provided postprandial delight for revelers in the great halls of Irish castles. He was as acolyte and disciple to the poet-seer who supplied him with stirring lines for memorization. As the musician is to the composer so is the *reacaire* to the poet. To recite is *to make present again*. A Vancouver poet once attended a poetry evening I gave in that city and called me later to ask if I would coach her in the recitation of her own poems. It took only one session, the beginning of a friendship, for her to grasp an essential key. I told her to: "Breathe deeply and become very relaxed. Recall the original idea or phrase that caught your imagination. What truth was being communicated to you? Give thanks for the mystery, love and wisdom that inspires you. Hold that focus as you recite."

The years I spent in Vancouver after my marriage ended, afforded me opportunities to present my evenings of poetry, song and story throughout British Columbia's breathtakingly beautiful province. I travelled to several outlying islands conducting workshops and giving performances. Once, following a presentation in Tofino, Vancouver Island, a young man came to thank me saying, "I have just returned from Indonesia where I spent the last year travelling. Do you know that although what you do is unusual, there are a few women over there who go from place to place raising consciousness, singing songs and telling stories in a similar way to you."

The memory of faces and places has a nostalgic edge. Rumi said: *Remembrance makes people desire the journey. It turns them into travellers*. Bard and *reacaire* were referred to as *rememberers*, cultivating a remarkable memory in the course of their travels. A rich tradition of chanted lays and epics, incantations, songs and rhymes was passed orally from one generation to another. The memory for words and faces is at the core, a heart-memory. The task of the mystic bard in the esoteric tradition was to present truths to society in a way in which they could be accepted, understood and assimilated, implying sensitivity to the spirit of the time, the *zeitgeist*. The bardic practitioner was also required to breathe new life into old songs, to acquire new repertoire on and for the road. The sagaman of the Finnish Kahlevala spoke certain words three thousand years ago which I believe express the impulse and purpose of the bardic tradition in every age.

> I am wanting, I am thinking
> To arise and go forth singing
> Sing my songs and say my sayings
> Hymns ancestral harmonizing
> Lore of kindred lyricking
> In my mouth the words are melting
> Utterances overflowing to my
> tongue are hurrying
> So that we may sing good songs
> Voice the best of all our legends
> For the hearing of our loved ones
> Those who want to hear them from us.

There is a need also to cultivate silence and careful attention to one's surroundings along the way. Ram Dass, an easternized American, tells the story of his first trip to India when his guru commanded him to go for a long trek in the mountains assigning him an enlightened young guide. From time to time he was beset by the temptation to impress his guide.

"Did I every tell you about the time I was in Mexico?" he inquired at one point.

"BE HERE NOW." Was the curt response, but the message was clear...

A Backward Glance

I had been a painfully shy child, shrinking from centre stage as the periwinkle from the pin. A nun who taught me in sixth grade told my mother that she had to refrain from asking me questions in class because my embarrassment was so acute it would even cause her to blush. It took me more than half a lifetime to overcome this handicap and to be less susceptible to praise and blame. Paradoxically I never showed any reluctance in singing solo, making my stage debut dressed as a sailor at age four in a kindergarten production of *The Doll's Wedding*. Competitive singing which went with the territory of convent schooling, steeled my nerves. I would endure anxiety and discomfort for the sake of winning a medal because success always won favor. At any rate I grew up with the idea that singing was a pleasurable and natural expression of heart. I never had the kind of voice that would warrant serious training but I soon found that singing in the Irish language, with all its soulful vowels, was what I loved and I began to listen keenly to tapes and records of the Connemara singers I wished to emulate. The first song I made my own was *Anach Cuain* one of the great death songs which the blind journeyman poet Raftery, had composed in the mid- eighteen hundreds, close to the town of my birth. I had just learned it when my father asked me for the first time to accompany him on his annual pilgrimage to Lough Derg in Donegal, otherwise known as *St. Patrick's Purgatory*. There he introduced me to the joys of penance he so eagerly inflicted upon himself. It was a rigorous three day routine of fasting, sleep deprivation and continuous bare footed circling of stone beds in the rain. All night church vigils, incessant prayer and those incidental foot reflexology treatments on sharp stone, produced signs of glowing health and high spirits in survivors who rowed back to the mainland purified and sanctified. We broke the long car ride home by stopping in a small town where a *feis* [festival of music and dancing competitions], was in progress. My father admonished me to jump up on the back of the lorry that was parked in the town centre as makeshift but customary stage. In my state of renewed holiness I sang out *Anach Cuain* to my heart's content. When I got back into the car I was the proud bearer of a little silver cup—the first prize. Since then it has been my father's favorite song.

Between the age of four and twelve I learned a lot from nuns, who were a great mystery to me. Ireland was full of nuns then. I heard of a young English boy who spent a holiday in our town. When he went home somebody asked him, "What did you see when you were in Ireland?"

"Nuns," was his reply.

Although I could not have articulated it at the time, nuns appeared representative of a gender neither male nor female. This was underscored by the fact that only a little bit of their faces was visible, elaborate headdress being a feature of the habit in those days. The life of a nun was deemed a noble calling to which one might justifiably aspire. Implicit in it was the guarantee of happiness in the next world. I was bent on more immediate rewards and felt no tremor of a vocation. Many of my schoolmates however toyed periodically with the notion of *entering*. At least one out of every class usually joined in the end and not necessarily the ones we had identified as 'holy'.

I remember one nun in particular who introduced me in a precise and unforgettable manner to the rubrics of English composition. Her religion classes were usually devoted to the theme of ***PURITY,*** the virtue associated with sexual restraint and held aloft in every convent. Reaching fever pitch one day she implored us to instruct our mothers to sew sleeves and skirts onto our bathing suits. The irony of all this was that very few of us had bathing suits or had ever seen a beach and it was unlikely that we would adorn the wind and rain swept strands of the Atlantic in any kind of scanty attire, then or later.

Most mornings she had us standing with arms outstretched reciting rosary after rosary with no hurry to get around to the *three Rs*. Later I learned that this used to be a common practice of Celtic Christian saints. In the sixth century St. Kevin of Glendalough had mortified himself by standing so long in this position, knee deep in freezing water that some birds had built their nest in his open palms.

A Love of Learning

When I was twelve my name appeared among the first hundred listed when the result of a nationwide examination in Irish was circulated. This won me a coveted place in one of the four or five preparatory colleges located in remote *Gaeltacht* [Irish speaking] areas around the country.

Thenceforth referred to as *ábhar múinteora* [the *stuff* of teachers] we were moulded to fit the national ideal, fluent in Irish, proficient in Latin, Catholic in orientation, well versed in the musical and literary Irish tradition with a good grasp of our history and mythology. It was expected, in return for a generous governmental subsidy, that we would pass our education on when we eventually assumed our secure and respectable positions as teachers.

Among the faculty at our college were authors of the text books we studied who would move on to distinguished university careers when this experiment of DeValera's government ended, as it did in my final year. Over half the students were drawn from the Aran Islands and Connemara to facilitate a total immersion in the Irish language. It became evident to me that a percentage of people in my country whose fluency in Irish arose out of a racial consciousness at once foreign, exciting and deep, spoke only the most halting English as a second language.

At the end of four years a few opted for university courses but the majority of us proceeded as planned to Teacher Training College, Irish continuing to be our preferred medium of expression. A division of interests began for me when I was given the leading role in an Irish opera performed in my final year of training. Tomás MacAnna, later artistic director of the Abbey Theatre, was in the audience on the opening night and invited me to do a drama course with him during the summer. This led to a stint at the Damer, a semi-professional Irish language theatre. *An Triail* [The Trial] was the main dramatic offering of the season with Fionnuala Flanagan (now a movie star) in the lead. Tomás, whom I later came to know well when he directed for my husband in Toronto, invited me to join the cast for the annual Christmas pantomime at the Abbey Theatre, which usually had a long run and which that year, included the celebrated actors Donal McCann and Stephen Rea. Before I could avail of this means of augmenting my teacher's salary by six pounds weekly, I had to acquire the approval of Earnán de Blaghd. A friend of President DeValera's, he maintained quality control of the Irish language in our national theatre. I sang a couple of *sean nós* [old style] songs for him. To my surprise he beckoned me over and proceeded to examine my ears and by the mystery of this yardstick I was hired. Maybe he had been influenced

Stars Above the Road

by the remark, 'the woman or the donkey who don't look at you with their ears are no good.'

It was in the course of this run that I encountered Robert O'Driscoll on the stairs of a house in Dublin where we both had rooms. I consequently forsook the Irish-speaking theatrical circle I knew for the more established academe, which intersected all factions of Dublin life. There was theatre to be found everywhere, and entertaining characters competed with each other in pub and drawing room. Social gatherings became the 'be-all and end-all' for me. Whatever one saw on stage had usually been enacted in real life first. No drama can grow out of anything other than the fundamental realities of life. I remember a lady of my acquaintance calling out in a voice that all could hear, during the interval of her recently estranged husband's new play "My lines are coming across very well." I grew up beside Tom Murphy, Ireland's leading playwright. A bus load of our townsfolk always arrived at the Abbey for a production of his, sure to know who amongst their ranks had inspired this character or that in the play, giving familiar traits universal relevance.

The Dublin social treadmill of those days was not for the faint of heart and was severely challenging to anybody with a regular job, leading to the frequent repetition of a remark of Oscar Wilde's about *work* being the curse of the drinking classes. But it was to be recommended in small doses for those with the stamina to endure high levels of merriment and indoor adventures of a mental kind. You could set out in good and sedate order with plans for an early night, attending a lecture or a Yeats play, proceeding afterwards to a pub for some scholarly discourse which might suddenly erupt into a sing song. Levels of conversation would rise in growing animation and soon a mood of carefree abandonment would sweep the room giving occasion for the barman's anxious cry over the din: "Have ye no homes to go to?" We would be shepherded out into the reality of the cold night air soon to be piling into cars, careening through highways and byways, because somebody had a friend somewhere who had a few bottles of whiskey and who could withstand an all night vigil. In those days you never got up to see the sunrise but often stayed up until the breaking of daylight brought the revels to a natural conclusion. A whole book might be devoted to these late night escapades and the stories that were embroidered out of them.

A classic tale emerged about writers Brian O Nualláin (whose brother married a sister of mine), Brendan Behan, and Patrick Kavanagh, who could not drink together in Dublin because one or other of them was barred from any given pub. They had the bright idea to hail a taxi and instigate a pub crawl beyond the confines of the city. At each watering hole they noticed a sinister figure in a corner, drinking what appeared to be a mug of tea. The sight of this solitary man gradually became a source of paranoia in one or all of them. Finally, now some twenty miles outside the city in a snug little bar, they approached him with the question: "Are you following us by any chance?" Innocently he looked at them—"Sure am n't I your taxi driver!" Yarns were the fruit of all such episodes and gave excuse for more rounds of social drinking. I was introduced in this manner to poetry, song and story in the fast lane, the pace of which was guaranteed to steer anyone towards an early grave. There was a wealth of oral tradition to be *imbibed* along the way, but anything gathered in a state of inebriation was liable to be lost to subconscious memory only.

During this period I lost my inhibition and found my voice. Lectures became a great source of enjoyment, no longer abstract when the speaker was known to one and passionate about his/her subject. Whatever theme was being sounded on the podium always seemed to be in context of some conversation to which I had been privy. I became aware of the importance of cultivating a natural style of delivery, and never sacrificing the engagement of an audience to the temptation of pedantic vanities. Irish academics are well aware of the entertainment value that must attend even the most serious of topics and they always add a good sprinkling of humor. Post lecture get-togethers were convivial and relaxed, a great hush fell when a song was called for and I was often put on the spot. It was in the warmth of these gatherings that I acquired the ability to sing from the heart in response to the receptive listening field that productive social encounter engenders.

My education had left me better prepared for the role of professor's wife than it had for the actual job I held during our two years of courtship. I had been plunged in at the deep end, my first day of school coinciding with that of 43 four-year-olds in search of a teacher.

Curriculum-driven and under imminent threat of an inspector's visit I, to my subsequent regret, subjected these little ones to a harrowing daily round of *Rs*, with only occasional pauses for games or artwork. I was not even aware at that point, of the need for special kindergarten training or that a science of pedagogy existed through which faculties other than cognitive and verbal ones could be developed.

Happily, I would discover Waldorf schools when our children were young but they were only twinkles in our eyes as yet.

Bob, as he was known, arrived in Dublin to teach at University College only months before we met. A high achiever from an early age, he and his great friend Pat O'Flaherty were the first graduates of Memorial University Newfoundland to be granted foreign scholarships. They opted to study at London University, both earning Ph.D. degrees. Bob procured his by the age of twenty three, an exploration of the work of Sir Samuel Ferguson, a Northern Irish Protestant who had declared, "I am an Irishman and a Protestant but I was an Irishman before I was a Protestant." Ferguson was a poet in the epic style, who laid the foundation for Yeats and others with the authenticity of his translations from the Irish. Having studied the language he avoided the stilted efforts of earlier translators and carried forward glimpses and gleams of a lost art, that Irish poets might learn again the wavering, unemphatic rhythms of the originals.

Ferguson's pioneering spirit found resonance in Bob, and his efforts to reconcile the religious differences of mid eighteenth century Ulster were often cited by my husband in lectures in which he pointed out that the struggle that had bedeviled Ireland for centuries was a fratricidal one, since Ulster Protestant and Southern Catholic shared a common cultural heritage. Ferguson had overcome a great aversion to Catholics when he began to comprehend the intricacy and sophistication of the literature in Irish. He had then substituted his litany of vices for the following virtues which Bob used to quote with relish. They were qualities anyone who knew him would ascribe to himself–

loyalty, hospitality, openheartedness, idealization of women, sanctity of place, love of tradition, a sense of wonder.

Bob applied for a job at Reading university in England and was put to work editing a Yeats' manuscript. This led him to Dublin and subsequently, for better or worse, to me. His most remarkable feature was the timbre of his speaking voice reminiscent for me of the quality of voice I had encountered among native speakers of Irish in Connemara. Newfoundlanders like Aran Islanders depended on the sea for their livelihood. The rough and unrelenting fierceness of the landscape was reflected in many of the Newfoundlanders I came to know, most particularly in the man I married.

Pat O'Flaherty, Bob's life-long friend wrote the following description in *Books Canada* when he died:

> *Soon after arriving in England, we found ourselves one evening in the main hall of University College London, where a debate was taking place on the possibility of European union. The debate was in its finals stages, would-be Ciceros were orating from the floor in the odd accents of the British upper class. I could hardly pick out what they were saying. I turned to speak to Robert (Bob), but he had left my side. A minute later he appeared on the dais in front of the hall, and proceeded to address an audience of about three hundred, in an accent that must have seemed as peculiar to them as theirs did to me, on the virtues of continental federation. He knew nothing about European union, but this did not stop him from expostulating on the issue, without preparation of any kind and at considerable length.*

Bob often spoke of himself as being "propelled by forces beyond myself," or "following the cry of the wind." Certainly to be in his company was to experience how the inevitable never happened but the unexpected often occurred. Any suggestion of injustice in the air had him drawing an invisible sword and racing off in defense of the

Treasa O'Driscoll

victims. Seeing some plain clothes policemen pull a young man by the ear and bustle him into a waiting car sent him charging James Bond-like after them to the Galway police station to demand an explanation for the event. He organized a strike amongst the holidaymakers on our bus in Turkey while we were on honeymoon, because it appeared that the tour operator had short-changed us. The money was all returned... Later that night instinct led him off the beaten track to a seedy district of Istanbul where we gate-crashed a circumcision party. The sounds of the muted revelry among a group of traditionally clad Turks had not escaped his attention as we went for an evening stroll. Never a dull moment...

Bob proposed to me hours after returning from a holiday in Rome. He, his close friend Lorna Reynolds and novelist Kate O'Brien, all speakers at an international conference, were the guests there of Darina Silone, Irish born wife of an important Italian writer. By coincidence my parents were in Rome, and he met them for the first time; the liking was mutual and Bob's great affection for my father grew over the years. We married a few months before he was due to begin teaching at St. Michael's College in the University of Toronto.

For a few years he confined himself to a painstaking preparation for lectures, while the arrival of two baby boys in quick succession gave me domestic focus. Life in Toronto seemed staid when compared with the hectic social round we had known in Dublin, where so many people excelled in being eccentrically themselves. But social convention in Canada was more conducive to family life. One could always rely on guests making a sober departure by midnight. But the normality of our household routine was short-lived.

No sooner had Professor Robert established himself as a lively and reliable teacher, sure to be in alert attendance at every faculty meeting, a natural favorite of students, a charming and, at that point, only a mildly outrageous asset to staff parties, than he proceeded to bring his unique leavening to bear on a predictable and flat mix of university affairs. He found many allies among the erudite and distinguished company of priests who were his colleagues and whose counsel he often sought. They lauded his successes and tolerated his excesses to the furthest reaches of compassion when, with the passage of time, he no longer functioned as an asset to the institution.

Our downtown house was a hub of artistic and cultural life that could quicken the equally hospitable core of St. Michael's College, presided over by John Kelly, a charismatic Irish-American Basilian priest, a beloved and abiding supporter of Bob's while his extra curricular activities at St. Michael's were attracting an estimated thirty-five thousand people. Bob pioneered North America's first comprehensive undergraduate program in Celtic studies, an innovative collaboration between universities on both sides of the Atlantic. He gave Canadian students the opportunity to explore the full range of Celtic civilization and learn Irish, Scot's Gaelic and Welsh, under the guidance of some of the most distinguished scholars in the field. It is a program that still thrives today.

Bob, in twenty years of indefatigable effort, succeeded in opening up the consciousness of North America to the Celtic continuum, the oldest living cultural and spiritual stream in Europe. This revival was effected in a series of

Treasa O'Driscoll

lively and memorable festivals of art and scholarship which were open to the general public. The first major festival, held in Toronto in 1978 gave the movement for Celtic renewal an international dimension with one of the two thousand participants coming from as far away as Persia. The book which emerged from this convention is entitled *The Celtic Consciousness*. Ever inclusive, Bob employed a diversity of scholarly approaches in producing this comprehensive exploration of the myth, music, history, literature, folklore, art and archaeology of the Celtic world and of the far reaching effects of this culture into contemporary life.

He appointed a Celtic Arts board of directors, drawing from the ranks of Toronto's high society, which included Catherine Graham, Adrienne Clarkson (Canada's current Governor General), Hilary Weston (Ontario's most recent Lieutenant Governor). The work of this board has continued beyond Bob's death under the effective chairmanship of one of Bob's foremost patrons, Dominican priest and historian Edward Jackman, who facilitated and funded the publication of *The Irish in Canada: the Untold Story*. This was a two-volume *magnum opus* of some one thousand pages, a prodigious undertaking of scholarly and social significance to which Bob devoted every ounce of available energy while pursuing a full time teaching career, manic episodes notwithstanding.

Buckminster Fuller, W.H Auden, Kathleen Raine, Siobhán McKenna, P.L. Travers, Tim Pat Coogan and every other guest of ours, paid tribute to my husband's remarkable energy and enterprise. Loudest of all in his praises was Joseph Campbell, who opened the 1978 conference. Marshall McLuhan, an academic who was secure enough in his own individuality to recognize greatness in a colleague, in introducing Professor Campbell pointed out that the unity of human consciousness and the recapitulation of many of the motifs which abound in Campbell's work were now actualized and celebrated in the events organized by Robert O'Driscoll.

We engineered the North American premiere of *The Chieftains* and nine Irish plays, including a legendry production of Sean O'Casey's *Juno and the Paycock*, directed by Sean Kenny and starring the incomparable Siobhán McKenna. These gave excuse for some of our most enjoyable after performance parties at our home in Summerhill Gardens. Paddy Maloney, Sean Potts and Martin Fay, the core of The Chieftains group, were known to me since my days in the Damer and I had sung a few songs with them on various occasions. It was a struggle to garner a small audience for their first Toronto gig. I remember the night they arrived from the airport. We wined and dined them until the small hours. After they repaired to their hotel I made some attempt to clear away empty bottles and glasses and airily tossed a piece of paper into the fire with cigarette ashes. I read it and laughed.

The O'Driscolls have sole rights to The Chieftains in North America, signed Paddy Maloney.

It would be another year before they acquired an assertive New York agent and began to truly blaze a trail throughout the world, developing in a way that only real genius does.

We maintained our connections with all our literary *spalpeens* (journeymen labourers) of the seventies during our annual summers in Dublin which extended to eighteen month sojourns every seven years. Marshall McLuhan, in his autobiography, mentions a memorable party we threw for him and his beautiful wife Corrine when they came to Dublin. A photograph of the legendary McLuhan appeared in the Sunday Press. In it he is crouching on the floor with Siobhán McKenna and her dog Rory. The caption reads *uproarious party*, because Rory barked incessantly while the revels continued until dawn. It was during one of these sojourns that the Irish recording company Gael-linn launched my *Farewell but Whenever,* Irish love songs in the sean nós style most of them sung in Irish. This gave rise to more parties and a memorable week in the luxury of Dublin's Gresham Hotel graciously provided by the record company.

My duties as hostess to many itinerant scholars and artists and the exigencies of rearing four children ensured that I had little time for reading during those twenty years. I acquired a unique education in a very natural way, gathering knowledge in the course of everyday life. Interesting and hectic as this way of life proved, it played against the backdrop of hospitalizations for Bob, growing in frequency as a bipolar pattern began to inexorably take root. Highly sensitive people are most susceptible to fear, an element of our collective soul life although we can learn to find within ourselves the depths of love that can cast fear out. Bob often talked about a very frightening experience he had as a child and somehow this event lived on in his subconsciousness. His delicate psychic balance had been severely disturbed by a near fatal car accident in which we were both involved in the late sixties. Injuries to his spine brought on erratic mood swings in the course of which he threw caution to the wind. Habits of excess in his nature became more accentuated. Only a sober and disciplined life could have provided the grounding he needed to have any hold on sanity. The so-called intellectual training upon which much of academe prides itself was thrust upon him at far too early an age—he entered university at age fifteen. Bob's leaning was predominantly artistic and there were rival compunctions at war within his very rebellious nature which erupted into wild states, invariably followed by depression. It is tempting to indulge in the analysis of other people's ways whose behavior we can witness, but not the experience that lies behind it. The unpredictable and exhausting demands of this illness eventually led me to seek refuge in therapy. I only gradually found the courage to abandon a situation that was beyond my power to change.

We made our last foray as a couple in July 1989, going on the insistent recommendation of a recent acquaintance to India, where Bob was convinced my intention of leaving him could be negated. I was still in search of the miracle that would restore equilibrium to our lives and could be easily persuaded to spend a month in the exotic environs of the Poona ashram of Osho Rajneesh, a guru previously unknown to either of us. Osho was soon to die and made a rare appearance on the full moon before a gathering of ten thousand white-robed swaying bodies among whom now numbered the O'Driscoll's. The first sannyasin who greeted us had inquired: "And whose parents are you?" But our children could not have seen the sense in coming so far in search of a healing which in hindsight might have been more readily found within more tightly knit family ranks. We enjoyed Osho's videotaped talks. A distinguished professor of philosophy Rajneesh, (previously known as Bagwan) whose student body was so huge that it could not be contained within any lecture hall, had found it necessary to give his talks in the open air. This bursting out of established structure had been Bob's invisible model for his own endeavors so Osho's style had struck a chord with him. This guru endeared himself to me on short acquaintance as one of the greatest storytellers the world has ever known. Sannyasins were always collecting jokes for him, many of them quite off color. A sheaf of the latest ones would be handed to him before a talk, he would take them all in at a glance and would then weave the most hilarious philosophical discourse around these yarns-a true phenomenon of memory and wit to turn the tables on all academic pedantry. It made me realize how much the philosopher and born comic have in common. We were invited to view the ashram's vast library which included a copy of Bob's *Celtic Consciousness*. Osho honored me also in requesting that I add a presentation of poetry and song to the many fine musical offerings from all over the world, heard nightly in the magnificent white marble floored Buddha Hall. We were initiated into the order of *White Brotherhood* at the guru's full moon celebration and given new names, *Ma Prabod Divya*, meaning *Celestial Awareness*, for me and for Bob *Love Beyond Desire*, in its Indian form, *Swami Vitkam*.

The nervous exhaustion and confinement endured on the long plane ride home brought on a severe manic episode in Bob, leading to the inevitable hospitalization. Paranoia was entrenched in him and every move of mine was viewed with suspicion. Five months after our return from India, I secured a legal separation, making the break with the support of friends. Bob's preoccupation with conspiracy theory was total by then. Fixed obsession was an obvious side effect of psychiatric drugs, copiously administered over years of affliction. Assailed by fearful foreboding as coming events cast their shadow in him, he exerted a monumental effort of concentration and financial risk in producing his *Armageddon* series, with such arresting titles as *Nato and the Warsaw Pact are One, The New World Order and The Throne of the Anti-Christ, Corruption in Canada*. Most of his research was conducted in bars where he was more and more frequently at home after I left him. He found refuge with the mad and marginalized, the heartbroken and oppressed in whom addiction or adversity had wrought its disconnection from the fullness of feeling, the essential human passage to healing. His truly compassionate nature and innate courage led him into the belly of the dragon from which he could ultimately find no means of escape. Many of the scenarios that robbed him of sleep as he inwardly lived through them, are ironically coming to pass in our world today and the limited editions of his Armageddon books are much sought after by conspiracy theorists. He fled from Canada in 1995 in fear of his life and spent a few restless months in Dublin, cared for by my sister Anne, until his spirit sought its eternal release on February 29, 1996. When someone enquired of me in Vancouver, shortly after his passing, if I had once been married to the O'Driscoll who wrote conspiracy books I replied, "No..., I was once married to the Robert O'Driscoll who wrote *The Celtic Consciousness.*" Our partnership, once fruitful, had ended when his attention no longer focused on Ireland. Despite his fall from public grace and the poverty and loneliness of his final tragic months in Ireland, he was a catalyst for renewal in my life and in the lives of many.

> Go, merciless man, enter
> into the infinite labyrinth of
> another's brain

Treasa O'Driscoll

> Ere thou measure the circle he
> shall run,
> Go, thou cold recluse into the
> Fires
> Of another's high flaming bosom
> And return uncondensed,
> and write laws
> If thou cans't not do this,
> doubt thy theories.
> From William Blake

> *Think where man's glory most begins and ends*
> *And say my glory was I had such friends.*
> W.B. Yeats

Five

HOUSEHOLD NAMES

George, the widow of W.B. once cautioned a Yeats critic who came to interview her, "Do not spend all your life on Yeats." A good deal younger than her husband she outlived him by some thirty years and had ample opportunity to observe the growing phenomenon of Yeatsian scholarship taken up with the fervor of a religious vocation by academics worldwide. My husband numbered among them and I was easily converted. Yeats studies were part and parcel of the life that opened up to me when I became engaged to Bob who was always, from the day I met him, at work on one manuscript or another. All arrangements between us from the beginning had to be laid before a Yeats tribunal. My husband's oft repeated favorite quotations soon lodged mantra-like in memory.

Whenever he proved obstinate in argument I could let the following line roll off my tongue: "Bob-didn't Yeats say at the age of eighty—I have felt the convictions of a lifetime melt in a moment—and here you are stubbornly refusing to concede a simple point..." His arsenal was more heavily loaded and if I ever suggested that he might begin to curb his workaholic tendencies he had the following quote at the ready:

"Excess is the vivifying spirit of the finest art and we must always seek to make excess more abundantly excessive."

Some of the finest minds and most delightful people were drawn to explore the labyrinths of wisdom Yeats had explored, the rich yield of interests he harvested in friendship with his peers.

His contemporaries had led him into the study of French symbolism, Rosicrucianism, the Upanishads, Japanese Noh, hermeticism, magic, mythology and folklore. This poet, dramatist, senator, and public man had moreover, an endless fascination with himself, his own moods and idioms. James Stephens had to ask about Yeats: "Has he the right to saddle carefree citizens with his politics, his aristocracy, his philosophy, his love affairs–all his whatnots?" before concluding that time would tell whether or not Yeats had hung around too often in his poems, endlessly clanked about in his rhymes.

Time brought something of a positive judgment to bear in the form of an annual Yeats Summer School to which aficionados flocked for two weeks every August, and which continues without a lapse since the early sixties. Bob was among the speakers and teachers for several years who approached the mecca of Sligo town and environs, ground hallowed by Yeats for all time, its litany of placenames sounding through the poems, Ben Bulben, Knocknarea, Innisfree, Lissadell, Dooney.

There was a great hush of expectancy as a speaker mounted the podium to deliver manna extracted from Yeats' comprehensive theory of aesthetics or from his fertile exchange with his contemporaries Ezra Pound, Rabindranath Tagore, Lady Greogry, AE, John Millington Synge, to name but a few. A great interplay of influences from past and present brought about the powerful self development that Yeats' genius demanded. There was endless speculation in the afternoon seminars on such topics as Yeats' epitaph and what he really meant by it.

Cast a cold eye on life
on death
Horseman pass by...

We traveled one by one to Drumcliff Churchyard to meditate upon these words or ponder the apocalyptic significance of an image from *The Second Coming*, that arresting *rough beast* that was *slouching towards Bethlehem to be born*. Bob would engage me for hours in his Sherlock Holmes like probing into these conundrums. He also liked to claim that our first son Briain was conceived at one of Yeats' favorite haunts. It is true that I gave birth nine months after the 1966 school and that his father had inserted *William Butler* into the child's name on the birth certificate, despite protests from me. Romance blossomed amongst the Yeats devotees, a certain licentiousness had the sanction of Yeats' purported sexual exploits in later life.

Yeats had worried about love, making it the source of passion and drama in his life, writing about it as if it were an "almost–crime" thought James Stephens, who conceded that the great poet approached love as a violent kind of thing "that doesn't really brood about chickens, but is passionately concerned about the mice." The extracurricular bed-hopping at the summer school would have done him proud. Crazy Jane's remonstrations gave them bold directive.

>...A woman may be proud and stiff
>When on love intent
>But love has pitched his mansion in
>The place of excrement;
>For nothing can be sole or whole
>That has not been rent.
>
>From Yeats, Crazy Jane Speaks with the Bishop

A Leaning Towards Riches and Fame

Love for the teacher is a great stimulus to the brain and my rapt attention during Bob's daily seminars would easily have earned me an A. All speakers and spouses gathered in Sligo's Imperial Hotel, an establishment once frequented by Yeats himself and at that time boasting the same fixtures and, some would argue, even the same mattresses as in Yeats' day. The speakers who had held forth that morning could bask in the reflected glory of luminaries such as Richard Ellmann, Northrup Frye and the director himself T.R. Henn, at the large round table in the dining room. It was there that I first became aware of the searching insight and poetic vision of Kathleen Raine who was a revered presence among us every year. I was much in awe of her then and held back, but she later honored me with letters of encouragement as Bob's illness progressed, always urging me to be happy in spite of circumstance.

Critical post mortems on the morning talks were conducted by the drinkers late at night. These were sessions I rarely enjoyed, alleviated by bursts of song, sometimes from scholars who could not hold a tune. Emotional immaturity often countered precocious intellect. To have a starring role in this scholarly exhibition was a mixed blessing; on the one hand, a recognition that one was amongst the elite and on the other, marking one a sitting duck for all the begrudgers present. I was led to understand that my naive enjoyment of the lectures was due to my lack of a critical faculty.

Most speakers came very well prepared. A more daring approach was adopted by Francis Warner, genius extraordinaire and the youngest ever don at St. Peters College, Oxford. He could be heard hammering away on his typewriter as the day of display of his dazzling erudition dawned. He and I struck instant rapport and he subsequently wrote a part for me in his first play which afforded me six weeks in Oxford with my second infant son. Robert would become an actor himself when he grew up having had his first whiff of greasepaint in the Oxford Theatre at the age of two.

Francis used to stay with us in our tiny Toronto apartment during my first pregnancy, launching forth from there into the city's high society, often with us in tow like poor relations. Millionaires were eager to host him and further their associations with the hallowed institution he represented. Building projects at St. Peters were funded through these channels. Ever dashing, Dr. Warner always dressed as did Bob, in finely tailored three piece suits, his jackets revealing a flash of crimson lining. Now he occupies the chair that T.R. Henn held at Cambridge University, and when he showed me round his Oxford house a few years ago, I noticed that the same siren red adorned the opulent bedroom he shares with his beautiful young wife. Glamour attends him ever—he was our first link with the rich and famous. Richard Burton or Lawrence Harvey filled in for him at Oxford whenever he made fund-raising forays abroad. As her poet chronicler, he gave vivid account of Elizabeth Taylor's fortieth birthday party. Proceeds from his plays were earmarked for the Samuel Beckett theatre he had promised his friend Sam he would build. To that end he engaged the services of another friend, Buckminster Fuller, who planned to suspend the building embryo-like underground. But this proposition was shelved when the initial excavation unearthed an abundance of skeletons of long dead parishioners beneath the quadrangle of St. Peter's college.

In 1970, I traveled with the Oxford cast to Edinburgh where we were listed in the festival fringe events. Affairs took a slightly dramatic turn in true Francis style, when the leading man who had taken up a teaching post in Southampton had to make the nightly journey to Scotland by helicopter. One evening his arrival was delayed and I was nudged onto the stage to entertain the waiting audience. There had been a great hue and cry about the nudity for which Francis claimed artistic license and that would also be a feature of subsequent plays by him. What we did not realize was that the police morality unit had chosen to infiltrate the audience that night. It was elected that I would appear on stage to throw the officers off track. Imagine their bemusement and perhaps disappointment, when all they could witness was a fully clothed woman singing traditional songs in the Irish language. They departed before Francis and the actor finally arrived! It was this production that led to our touring the U.S. by which time Alan Schneider, Beckett's favorite director, had joined the team and we added *Come and Go* and *Breath* to our repertoire.

A Family Lunch

Michael Yeats inherited his mother's level-headed practicality and his marriage to Gráinne, daughter of the nationalist historian, P.S. O'Hegarty, has led to a fundamental shift in the Yeats lineage from Anglo to native Irish roots. With a house set in the Connemara *gaeltacht*, theirs is an Irish speaking household and Michael shares a musicological interest in traditional music with his wife, an accomplished harpist and singer. As executor of his father's estate he is endlessly patient in his shrewd handling of the demands of Yeatsian scholars, besides pursuing an international career in politics. As one who has had greatness thrust upon him, he appears to take it with a grain of salt. When I first heard him speak publicly in Sligo, he began with a story about a remark overheard when two locals in a rural town were reading a notice which said, *Lecture on Yeats*. Speculating that it might be some new class of vegetable, one said to the other, "What, do you suppose, is a *Yeat*?" They pronounced the name to rhyme with *beet* as many country people do.

Both Gráinne and Michael and his sister Anne, who celebrated her fifty sixth birthday in our home, became good friends of ours. They admired Bob's drive and his eagerness to include them in many of his extravaganzas. He once lured Gráinne and Anne to Toronto along with Jo and Liam Miller of the Dolmen Press, that they might confer together on the ideal mounting of a production of W.B. Yeats' Cuchulainn cycle of plays. James Flannery, renowned both as a fine tenor and for his work on Yeats' drama, was their unanimous choice of director. James bore the brunt

Treasa O'Driscoll

of Bob's maverick ways, having to coordinate a multimedia production that was top-heavy with celebrities. The natural diplomacy of Gully Stanford, Bob's able executive, who had forsaken Classics at Oxford to pursue a theatre career in Toronto, often saved the day. Bob would periodically intervene to stir up some issue of contention amongst cast members. "He seemed to revel in setting the cat among the pigeons and then take perverse delight in sorting out the mess himself," James recalled when I saw him recently in Atlanta.

I shall never forget my first visit to Michael and Gráinne's Dublin home. Bob had been on tenterhooks since the invitation to lunch with them on December 23rd 1972 was issued, and I was often reminded of the important event that lay ahead of us. I went to bed early the night before, not waiting up for Bob who was dining with Lorna Reynolds, his collaborator on the *Yeats Studies Journal*. The evening marked the onset of a paranoid episode – his first of many. I was not aware as I slept soundly upstairs, that he made his entry into our house by crashing through a basement window, sustaining in Houdini fashion, only a few small cuts. This was his way of evading the enemies he imagined were pursuing him. His behavior appeared very odd the next morning and he would not hear of my cancelling the appointment. With great apprehension I boarded the bus for Dalkey with him. When we arrived we found the entire Yeats family, Michael, Gráinne, their four children and Anne seated at a round, highly polished dining room table. We were late and they were about to start without us. Bob took his chair without a word glaring at everyone in sullen silence as bowls of dark oxtail soup were set before us. As I put a spoonful to my mouth he

Stars Above the Road

hissed, "Treasa, don't drink the soup." With a nervous laugh I improvised, "Oh that's right I'm allergic to oxtails." I am sure Michael was wondering was this the same professor who had badgered him with letters over the years, a person who had not appeared to be short of words. I made self-conscious attempts at small talk until a large chocolate mousse was placed in the centre of the table. Nobody could have known that on that day anything *brown* signified enemy action for Bob. With a decisive leap he bounded across to my side of the table pulling me swiftly to my feet and out the door declaring "Well that's it. My wife and I have had quite enough, thank you all very much!" I looked back upon bewildered Yeats faces as I gestured soundless apologies. There was more drama to follow before Bob was carried off in an ambulance by men in white coats later that night. Anne and Gráinne were present in publisher Liam and Jo Miller's house when another storm erupted a few years afterwards but they were well used to Bob by then, never doubting the integrity that lay behind erratic behavior. Both were particularly kind to me when they found me in tears afterwards.

James Stephen's account of a visit he paid the poet endears Yeats to me, coping as I write with this damp and draughty climate, without benefit of central heating.

> *"About a year before his death I went to his hotel, and was shown up to his bedroom. The great poet was in bed, with a dressing gown about him and a writing pad on his knee. We talked for a little, and then he said thoughtfully: "All my life I have been bothered as to how writers get on with their work in winter. If," he went on, "if you sit at a table and you get stiff hands and frozen feet, and then the stuff you write can only be warmed by sticking it into the fire."*

I agreed that, barring being boiled alive, being frozen to death was the worst torment of a literary life. "But," said Yeats triumphantly, "I've found out how to conquer cold feet. My feet are never cold now. Come over to the bed Stephens," he said, "and I'll show you."

He threw the coverlets off. He was fully dressed under the bedclothes, and had a dressing gown on over his ordinary clothes. But it was his legs that delighted me. "There," he said, "you can't get cold feet if you wear these." He had on a pair of huge rubber fisherman's boots that reached to his thighs. "Inside these," he said cunningly, "I have on a pair of wooly slippers, and I'm as warm as toast."

Making a Hero out of Joyce

James Joyce occupied centre stage in our household from time to time, particularly in February 1982. My husband, with the assistance of my brother Tomás Hardiman and a team of students, mounted a festival to celebrate what would have been the great man's hundredth birthday, February 2, the Celtic feast of *Imbolc* and *Bridget*, goddess-cum-Christian saint. Joyce had a superstitious attachment to dates of the calendar, not least his birthday and he would, I think, have approved of the revels that erupted in Toronto. To an admirer he once said, "Don't make a hero out of me. I'm only a simple middle class man."

Although he wrote the book that is as he predicted, keeping the professors busy for generations, I found that many of his ardent followers who surfaced during the festival were otherwise unburdened by learning. It was fitting that his *ordinary* readers abounded in our audiences, the kind of people Joyce has designated the true authors of *Ulysses* which he said "was written by those I have met or known."

He was referring to the undistinguished company of tailors, waiters, fruitsellers, hotel porters, bank clerks from whom he garnered his treasury of phrases. When an Irish relative complained that it was not fit to be read Joyce had retorted "If Ulysses is not fit to be read, life is not fit to be lived." Some of Joyce's fans, I observed, took a voyeur's delight in Joyce's sexually explicit references and could quote verbatim lines from Joyce to his wife Nora that displayed a fetish for her underwear. Many of the academics however, idealized the relationship between James and Nora, fascinated that their idol could have elevated so lowly a person, saying of her "No human being has ever stood so close to my soul as you stand." Nora was unschooled but had a rare gift of being natural and always herself in a world of literary posturing. Her direct and spontaneous speech lent authenticity to her husband's writings.

A hundred cares, a tithe of troubles might have been Joyce's epitaph for himself and Nora. Their nomadic existence across Europe was beset by sickness and poverty. Demons dogged Joyce in the form of drink, debts, publishers and chronically failing eyesight, his deepest source of grief being the apparently incurable mental illness of his lovely daughter Lucia, for which he blamed himself. The shadows of some similar troubles have been sufficiently cast over my own later married life for me to have developed deep empathy for the life the Joyces led.

John Cage's *Roaratorio,* an acoustic interpretation of Finnegans Wake, was a high point of the festival. Cage had sent technicians all over the world gathering up the aural phenomena referred to in the book, the cry of a newborn in Dublin's Hollis St. Hospital, snippets of songs or the shrieking of seagulls over the rock of Gibralter. The

Treasa O'Driscoll

technical challenges of wrapping a cacophonous soundscape around an audience in the university's circular Convocation Hall while Cage simultaneously intoned the text, would have daunted a impresario less daring than Bob. The avant garde composer also randomly conducted fragments of tunes by Irish traditional musicians who were on hand at enormous expense along with the Canadian percussion group Nexus. "Sing anything you like for no longer than twenty minutes when I beckon," Cage had instructed Seosamh O'hEanai, known also as *the king of song*.

On the following evening I took part in a concert which included Irish traditional musicians Liam Og O Floinn, Paddy Glackin, Seamus Tansey and Mel Mercier, all chosen by Cage for his production. An album entitled *Bloomsday* was later compiled from the singing and speaking of the great Connemara storyteller/singer Seosamh O'hEanaí and myself on that occasion. Jim Sheridan, later the director of *My Left Foot*, then an unknown genius at large, was living at the time in Toronto and a frequent visitor at our house. Sorel Etrog, foremost Canadian sculptor and dear friend, wrote a piece entitled *Dreamchamber* which Jim and I performed in Convocation Hall. It evoked the creative and iconoclastic climate of the period when Joyce and the Dadaists lived, for us *reacaires* it constituted an exercise in speaking mumbo-jumbo and keeping a straight face as we enunciated such a passage as the following, said to feature the longest word ever printed, a mixture of English and Irish:

Pappapapapparrassannuaragheallachnatullaghmonganmacmacmac-whackfalltherdebblenonthedubblandadadddydoodledand

There was so much talk about James Joyce in our house at that time that when a neighbor, film maker Joyce

Wieland, happened to call to the door one day, my little daughter aged five emerged from behind me to shyly enquire "Not *James* Joyce?" I enjoyed Cage's visits to our home, once in the company of Merce Cunningham and always with his basket of macrobiotic delicacies in hand. He memorably said of Bob, "He takes the '*im*' out of impossible and puts the '*in*' into infectious."

My love of Joyce led to encounters with some remarkable people. Joseph Campbell pronounced my interpretation of a few passages from *Finnegans Wake* as music to his ears, when he attended a performance I gave in New York. Anthony Burgess also voiced his approval when he heard me recite at a conference in Cork. The third intellectual heavyweight of this famous trio who had intuitively cut their critical teeth on the complex substance of the *Wake* was Marshall McLuhan. A colleague of Bob's at St. Michael's College and a champion of all his efforts on behalf of Irish studies, *Finnegans Wake* was prominent on his teaching curriculum and he often invited me into his classes to read or recite passages. He and his wife Corrine were very dear to us and they were always concerned for Bob's health. Once when he had been taken into hospital from the university I phoned Marshall to break the news to him. He listened compassionately and then said: "Now we will hang up and I will kneel down and say the rosary for Bob." A convert to Catholicism, a deeply Christian perspective lay behind his pronouncements on the culture of the day. Ironically this guru of communications was struck dumb for the last year of his life, having suffered a stroke. Two nights before his death he indicated his desire to visit the O'Driscolls. The whole family sat around our dining room table wondering how much the benign, smiling Marshall now understood of our thoughts and feelings. Some weeks later we all met again, joined by a Basilian priest friend, Fr. Schook and Sorel Etrog, to lay a plaque on his grave. It read *The truth will set you free.*

The guest I found most endearing of all over the years was Eileen O'Casey, widow of Sean, who once lectured around Ontario and made our house her base for several weeks. In her late seventies and overweight she was one of the most beautiful and glamorous women I had ever encountered. Possessed of a flawless complexion, every fleeting expression registered on her mobile features. Content to bask in her husband's reflected glory during his lifetime, she had star presence and was charismatically herself in every gathering. She evoked peals of laughter in the hilarious slant she had on every event of the day. We were so in tune that I was once taken for her daughter during one of our shopping forays in Toronto.

AE Enters with Mary Poppins

We did not encounter many contemporary followers of the mystic AE, who was as prominent a figure in Ireland as Yeats was, at the turn of the twentieth century.

AE lived according to a vision he had of a greater life saying: "I know that the golden age is all about us and that we can if we will, dispel that opacity and have vision once more of the ancient beauty." A very practical man who led the farmers cooperative movement, he frequently painted the fairies he saw in the woods.

Bob had devoted much study to the vision of AE and for a time a painting entitled *Meeting with a Celestial Being* by AE hung on our wall. His spirit only truly entered when Pamela Travers, author of *Mary Poppins* came to stay. She described herself as an apprentice *file* [poet] to AE at a time when he was growing old and she was as yet a young woman. They shared a sense of the secret but communicative life of trees and when she, an Australian, came to visit him in Ireland, AE would take her with him into the woodland, setting up his easel where he felt the strongest vibrations. And even though AE protested, "It is not now my time to burst into leaves and flowers" he was a prolific artist who completed at least one canvas every week of his life.

Mrs. Travers told our children about Mary Poppins but regaled us adults with her memories of AE of whom she never tired of talking. She told us of the weekly evenings in his home where fellow writers came to drink from his generous chalice of conversation. She read us her favorite passage from AE's *Candle of Vision*.

> ...I need not seek, for what was my own would come to me. I knew that all I met was part of myself and that what I could not comprehend was related by affinity to some yet unrealized forces in my being... There is no personal virtue in me other than this, that I followed a path all may travel but on which few do journey... None need special gifts or genius. Gifts! There are no gifts. For all that is ours we have paid the price. Genius is not bestowed but won...

I recalled my own favorite saying of AE:

> It is part of my philosophy that things that are evil are to be got rid of by thinking of their opposites. We become what we contemplate and human energy always operates through the image that is most present in consciousness.

Pamela Travers told us how AE had sent for her when he was dying in Bournemouth and how she cared for him and brought other friends to say a last farewell. She noticed that the full moon reflected the sun on its Northern journey on the night he died, a sign the Bhagavad Gita had given to mark the passing of a great spirit.

Treasa O'Driscoll

Some years later I stayed at Pamela Travers' Chelsea home and was amused to hear her housekeeper remark of the self portrait of A.E., on the cover of a biography of him I was reading: "Oh that is the gentleman who often stands behind the rocking horse in the hall!" She didn't know his name but she recognized the ghostly likeness in the picture. My hostess made me promise before I left that when I returned to Ireland I would go with my husband to Mount Jerome cemetery and then report back to her on the current state of AE's grave. We found him buried amongst 275,000 others, his grave overrun with weeds. Bob began a campaign to restore this sacred burial ground. Soon money poured into the fund from many of the friends and acquaintances of the great man who were still living, including Lord Moyne, Lord Dunsany and Monk Gibbon who had been a young protegee of AE's and who had written a poem as a tribute to the rare spirit who had brought so many to the realization of their own divinity.

> I have known one great man,
> One man alone to rise
> Shoulder and head above
> All his contemporaries...

With the help of his friends Maurice Henry and Anthony Cronin, Bob succeeded in raising enough money to erect a bust of AE in Merrion Square and to surround his grave with fine green Connemara marble. He was in daily contact with Pamela Travers and together they decided on the following epitaph to be carved upon AE's headstone:

> *I moved among men and places, and in living I learned the truth at last. I know I am a spirit, and that I went forth in old time from the self-ancestral to labors yet unaccomplished.*

The literati and glitterati were there for the unveiling of the headstone, the occasion marked by Anthony Cronin's reading of a passage from the Bhagavad Gita as instructed by Pamela. It had been a lovely sunny day and many were out in their finery. However at the mention of the word *rain* the heavens had opened and the assembled gathering had to run for cover to the nearest pub, where a generous American friend provided refreshments for all and sundry. A very old woman emerged from the shadows of the pub to inquire of me if the celebration had anything to do with "a man who lived some years ago by the name of AE," explaining that her sister had been his housekeeper. Her face was aglow as she extolled his virtues and his kindness to her entire family, so vivid was her memory of him that one could hardly believe that fifty years had elapsed since he had passed away. I took her appearance as a sign that the beneficent being we were honoring recognized our intentions.

AE visited America a few times at the request of the government as an advisor on the question of rural civilization. He greatly impressed the experts in Washington. Monk Gibbon reports: "On his last visit there, a question arose in a Washington discussion on the contest that was then raging between property rights and personal rights. He reached for a piece of paper and pencil and said he thought he could 'make a poem' about that, scribbling on it some lines.

> All that fierce talk of thine and Mine,
> If the true Master made His claim
> The world he fashioned so divine?
> What could they answer did He say
> "When did I give My world away?"

Treasa O'Driscoll

Yeats and AE had been influenced by the American transcendentalist movement in formulating their ideals for a Celtic Literary revival. The interplay of magic, mysticism, cosmology and mythology in their work and in Joyce's in a less obvious way, had a metaphysical underpinning. My immersion in the creative imagination and life stories of these great writers was my introduction to eastern and western esoteric traditions and the spiritual guidance inherent in them for every seeker. Shortly after Pamela's task was accomplished, I began to study Rudolf Steiner's spiritual scientific writings. Meanwhile, Bob and I, at Ms. Travers request, had gone in search of a specific translation of the Bhagavad Gita, that of the American Theosophist William Q. Judd. We did not find it in the library of the Irish Theosophical Society although we engaged there in lively exchange with alert older members of the society. We were eventually led to a retirement home where we met Miss Emerson, former teacher at Alexandria College, a posh Protestant girl's school. She was a direct descendant of Ralph Waldo Emerson. Then in her nineties she was as lively as a spring chicken. She had the coveted translation and could pinpoint the passage which Pamela instructed we read at the graveside unveiling. Bidding her a fond farewell we left the building.

"Bob," I said, "I want to be like her when I am old. I shall become a theosophist!"

The longer one studies life and literature the more strongly one feels that behind everything that is wonderful stands the individual, and that it is not the moment that makes the man but the man who creates the age.
Oscar Wilde

Six

A LINGERING PRESENCE IN TORONTO

Seán Ó Riada, a composer who lived from 1931 to 1971, was the outstanding artistic figure in the Ireland of his time, his music capturing the imagination of a whole nation. Seán Ó Mórdha, who made him the subject of a posthumous television documentary, wrote in The Irish Times:

Learned and stylish, his presence could transform the most mundane occasion into a memorable and celebratory happening. His boyish sense of humor—a concoction of word play, literary parody and outrageous role-playing—could keep a gathering in hoots of laughter throughout a leisurely afternoon.

I experienced the pleasure of hearing him live for the first time in Kilkee, County Clare, during the Merriman Summer School of 1970. His wife Ruth, who would herself die at a young age, introduced me to Seán after the concert. He took a step backwards when I held out my hand to him and he later told me that he experienced a shock of recognition on seeing me. The meeting led to my husband's invitation to Seán to participate in a forthcoming conference to be held in Toronto in February 1971. This conference would mark the dual centenaries of painter Jack B. Yeats and John Millington Synge. Seán's eagerness in accepting overrode his reluctance to "cross the Atlantic in an aeroplane" and his amusement at the smallness of the fee being offered to all participants. "I wouldn't blow my nose for $150 but I will come anyway!" I agreed to sing a few songs in the course of the concert. Letters were subsequently exchanged and, because he took such boyish delight in long distance telephone calls, he unraveled the few uncertainties relating to the final program with me over the wire.

He arrived in the company of Anne Yeats. Toronto seemed to live up to his expectations. His fear of flying furnished him with a legitimate excuse for high spirits. He thus engaged me, when I deposited him in his hotel, in the first of many long chats into the small hours. The brilliant carpet of snow, spread in welcome before him, the cosmopolitan air of the city and the hooley-like (Irish party) atmosphere that surrounded the social events of the conference, all contributed to his sense of having come from home to home.

He sat restless, through the opening panel discussion on the theme of the conference, *Theatre and the Visual Arts*, itching to add his insights to those of W.H. Auden, Buckminster Fuller, Marshall McLuhan, and Jack MacGowran. Had an opportunity afforded itself, he undoubtedly would have had much to add to the closing exchange between Auden and McLuhan.

> *Auden: Tradition means giving votes to that obscurist class, our ancestors. It is the democracy of the dead. Tradition refuses surrender to the small arrogant oligarchy of those who merely happen to be walking around.*
>
> *McLuhan: This is what old Agnew calls the silent majority?*

Seán whispered in my ear, "Auden stole that line from Chesterton." He knew about the democracy of the dead having apprenticed himself to the native carriers of language and oral tradition, some of them of advanced age, living around him in West Cork. He had moved with his family ten years earlier to the Munster Gaeltacht [Irish speaking district] settling down in the little village of Cúil Aodha, thus ensuring the continuity of cultural heritage, now quite foreign to urban Ireland, for his *seven generations thence.*

Upon observing that I sang as "a person singing a song and not as a *singer*" and that I had "the kind of mind that works in Irish," he extended me the full measure of his charm and wit, which cast its certain spell upon me. We spent less of the little time at our disposal practicing, in the accepted sense of the word, for the concert, than we did in exploring our mutual love of poetry and yarns. My choice of songs were all, by coincidence, favorites of Ó Riada's – *An Droighneán Donn, Liam Ó Raghallaigh, Brídín Bheasach*, he being drawn, as I am, to those moving expressions of unrequited love that began to assume a certain poignancy as we became aware of our deep attraction for one another. His sensitive chording reminded me, at every turn, of the essential meaning of the words I was singing and of the power of these melodies to embody the emotions that gave rise to them. My part in the concert was slight, because it was Ó Riada the audience wanted to hear, and hear him they did for something like three and a half hours.

Seán established and maintained a jolly rapport with the crowd, subduing it completely in the first few bars of *Marbhna Luimní*, the tune that a lone piper was to play at his own funeral later in the year. The composer Carolan and the Irish language vision poets of earlier centuries were all affectionately referred to in the course of his introductions as though they were dear personal friends. He played *Port a Phúca* as a composer, conveying to chilling effect the ghostly quality of the tune his friend Paddy Daly, alone in his hut on Inishvickillaun, had overheard late at night, as the elements pitched themselves in eerie harmony with the wild Atlantic.

The audience were allowed to draw their parallels between *Anacreon* (by Carolan) and the *Star Spangled Banner* and could not fail to hear echoes of *God Save the Queen* in *Robin is my delight, Ochone, Ochone*. But he was deadly serious when he proposed *Mo Ghile Mear* as an appropriate national anthem for Ireland, conveying a sense of courage and daring in the playing of it, alternating between harpsichord and piano (a benefactor, Frederick Eaton, had put one of the best grand pianos in the city at our disposal; consequently the harpsichord was left almost entirely abandoned during the concert). *Aisling Gheal* [bright vision] was introduced by him as "a song from my own parish" and elicited from him a story which I will quote, in his own words:

"I once saw a vision when I was twenty-one years old. I was walking home from Kilmalloch in County Limerick. I really did see a vision, a most frightening thing. I had come from Dublin on the train which stopped at Kilmalloch. No buses were running. As usual, I was not in agreement with my parents, so they hadn't sent a car. When you go outside Kilmalloch, a long straight road stretches in front of you so that you can see clearly ahead for two miles. I had been walking for about fifteen minutes when suddenly I saw a woman coming towards me - she hadn't been there a second before. She was wearing a long red skirt, a white blouse and had a shawl around her shoulders. The hair stood up on the back of my head. I was terrified. As she passed me, I followed her round like a magnet. Suddenly she wasn't there anymore. That, I think, was a real vision, a real aisling."

He talked about his admiration for the poet Raftery who played Irish music with his face to the wall at a time when it was not fashionable. "I feel if one is living at all, if one is really living, one must be living with passion and Raftery was dominated by a real passion and love of life."

His remark that laughter is the enemy of passion was counter-pointed by his altering the rhythms of such slow airs as *Bean Dubh a Ghleanna* to incorporate dance rhythms before returning to the original tempo he started with. He pointed out the Irish propensity of taking life with a grain of salt.

"You must learn to laugh at your own emotion," he declared.

He had the audience join him in *Óró Bog Liom í*, ("I hope we won't all be put out for singing obscene Gaelic songs in Canada.") *Róisín Dubh* was requested many times. He began by playing the version he had first heard his mother sing as a child "not for patriotic reasons but for local parochial reasons" before going on to do full justice to the song he

Treasa O'Driscoll

made famous in the *Mise Éire* score. He made reference to his mother's singing of *The Suit of Green* and played it after reciting the words. A last call for *one of your own* brought the response: "No... I'll play you one of my father's—a lullaby he sang me, my earliest childhood memory, in the hopes that you will either go to sleep or go home." And thus the concert finished in moving tribute to his father with *Bog Braon don tSeanduine*.

As the conference progressed, the kitchen of our house became the centre of action late at night, Ó Riada deciding to forsake his elegant hotel surroundings for a couch in our living room, all other nooks and crannies of the house being already occupied by guests. Not much time was devoted to sleep in any case. Claude Bissell was President of the University at the time. He and his Scottish-born wife Christine were famous during his fifteen-year term of office for their innumerable, stylish parties free of academic constraint. Claude mentions only two in his memoirs, one that was carefully planned as a surprise to honor Marshall McLuhan on his return from the United States in 1968; the other party that erupted suddenly. This was the reception they held after the opening of *The Heart's A Wonder*, Maureen Charlton's adaptation of *The Playboy of the Western World*. In his book, *Halfway up Parnassus*, President Bissell described this wild event.

> *It seemed as if a good part of the Toronto Irish community came to the house, and a fair number stayed on until first light, as if they were attending an enormous wake. We shall always remember gentle Seán Ó Riada, composer of austere, Schonbergian serialist music, fervent Irish nationalist, sitting at a battered piano in the recreation room, playing his Irish folk tunes while the hours rolled away and a mound of cigarette butts formed at his feet.*

Seamus Heaney recalls another occasion in a poem:

> ...As he stepped and stooped to
> the keyboard he was our Jacobite,
> he was our young pretender
> who marched along the deep
> Plumed in slow airs and
> grace notes...

The day of his departure was fraught with tragic glee. The actor Jack MacGowran, not long for this world either at the time, was unwell and held court from his hotel bed. Anne Yeats, James Flannery, Bob and I, along with John Richmond (the Literary Editor of the Montreal Star with whom Seán discoursed mainly in Greek) and Ó Riada positioned ourselves around the bed. Plans were hatched for the mounting of the Yeats plays in Toronto, which my husband would produce and for which Anne Yeats would design the sets, Ó Riada write the music, with Jack MacGowran directing them "six inches above the ground".

Such diversions were indulged in as the telephoning of the Prime Ministerial residence of Pierre Elliott Trudeau "just say that Seán Ó Riada called". Plans to rendezvous with Seán Kenny and Siobhán McKenna in New York, enroute to Shannon, were shelved, as the fun continued. The piece of music he had agreed to write for *Here Are Ladies,* Siobhán's one-woman show had, he said, regrettably been lost in the snow. No doubt it had been completed in his head, but the brilliance of the snow had diverted him from the actual writing down of the music for the moment. He wept when his departure could be delayed no longer, and we all had a sense of the party's being over. In a subsequent letter to my husband he toyed with the notion of putting an ad in a Toronto newspaper in which he might express his delight in the luxuriance of the

Treasa O'Driscoll

snow, the warmth of the people and the happiness his brief visit had afforded him.

He frequently called me from Cork and we exchanged letters. Most of the calls were short conveying only his "urgent need to hear your voice." Our next meeting took place in Galway two months later, where Dr. Lorna Reynolds had arranged a concert. Ó Riada was the star attraction. Seán Mac Donncha and I contributed a couple of songs. The accompaniments were truly delightful and I realized that because he knew the words of the old songs, their meaning was naturally relayed into every melismatic nuance.

Sometime during the concert, Seán's close friend, Garech de Brún arrived. Garech is owner of Claddagh Records and his entourage on this occasion included Paddy Maloney, of The Chieftains. Paddy sprang nimbly up on stage at Seán's invitation. A good-natured rapport between piano and tin whistle developed into something of a competitive joust.

I was also present at the last concert he gave, in Liberty Hall on 14th July—Bastille Day. Like Joyce, he had an exaggerated attachment to certain dates of the calender. He presented himself on stage that night in deference to his audience, the car crash three days earlier from which he had walked away having spat out most of his teeth on the road, notwithstanding. Had critics realized the pain he was in, they would have been more kind in their reviews. His shattered appearance and his despair were evident later that night when we could spend some time alone. The implications of an enforced liquid diet now marked the beginning of the end for him.

He celebrated his fortieth birthday on August 1, 1971. It was to be his last. He arranged recording sessions soon after for his final album, *Ó Riada's Farewell,* to coincide with my last days in Dublin before I would return with my husband and children to Toronto. When I saw him in the Shelbourne Hotel I was shocked by his gauntness. It was clear that he was very ill. I sat with him in his room and sadness filled the space between us. We were startled by a very loud knock on the door but when I looked outside there was nobody in the corridor. "It is the knocking on the door," he said, "my time is not far off," referring to one of the traditional warning signs of imminent death in a family. I was regrettably too young and too absorbed in my subjective feelings to speak the words of consolation he needed to hear.

Many of his works are permeated by the pathos which had often overwhelmed him when he sensed that time was running out for him. His greatest fear, confessed to me, was that he had lost his musical gift and would no longer compose. My presence in his life during his last few months had brought a ray of hope, the brooding images had turned to dreams of a happier future, in which we were transported into another reality. That could only be the stuff of dreams because we were both firmly committed to our marriages and families. He was the first man with whom I experienced a true soul communion that belonged more to eternity than to our short intimacy on earth.

> Set me as a seal upon your heart,
> As a ring upon your arm;
> For love is strong as death...
> Its flashes are flashes of fire,
> A flame of the eternal
> > Song of Songs (V111, 6-7)

That he was a man of many masks has been revealed in the various accounts by his friends since his death. The late Seán White described him to me as "the André Gide of our student days in Cork." Film maker George Morrison, whom I met once, remarked on the Edwardian pose he often struck so effectively in manner and dress.

A man sitting in the Ó Riada kitchen after the funeral was overheard by John Montague to say:

> *"Ah sure, we were nothing at all until he came along. He was our great Chieftain, our great Chieftain."*

He was indeed buried as a chieftain of old, his funeral procession stretching for miles as though he himself had stage-managed the ritual. His propensity in life to function as a kind of barometer in sensing or in altering the mood of a group at large, pronounced him a natural leader. He had access to corridors of power. Being a natural aristocrat, he could transcend all social barriers. He felt a sharp personal pain in the divisive forces sundering Northern Irish society—any threat to his country was experienced as a threat to himself.

He was the first Irish composer in a century of major writers to capture the imagination of a whole people. He knew, as Yeats did, that the literature of Ireland sprang from the rhizome of an oral culture in which music and speech were interdependent, the ancient music being our language where language ends. As Yeats was drawn to Celtic myth and mysticism, and as Synge discovered the life of the Aran Islands to be the outward expression of his inner being, so was Ó Riada drawn to Cúil Aodh in West Cork. Synge sights a moment of epiphany in his life when *everything Irish became precious and had a charm that was neither quite human nor divine, rather perhaps as if I had fallen in love with a goddess.* Ó

Riada had his own vision to which he attached a significance of similar magnitude. When he turned to what he termed the rich and comparatively untouched pastures of Irish traditional music, he was responding to his own spiritual needs. He clearly understood the centrality of the Irish language to the musical idiom he sought. He knew, as P.H. Pearse did, how close the unseen powers have always been to Irish-speaking men and women. He too aspired to the true Irish mysticism of Pearse, the mysticism which recognizes no substantial divide between seen and the unseen reality. When his commitment to his vision was total, he sought an exterior landscape and environment, as artists often do, which might reflect his own psychic geography and keep him close to those nerves of ancient tradition his creative alchemy might transmute into patterns that would always sound to Irish ears recognizable and at the same time, strange. In him, man and artist were one in his lifelong struggle to reconcile the diverse leanings of a rational nature with an instinctive return to all that was pure and rooted in Irish tradition. He demonstrated in this return, as only a great man could, that a man without a community behind him is no great man at all. His preoccupation with spiritual matters, his brooding about death, became more marked in the last months of his life.

Because he understood the intimacy with which Christ and Mary have been incorporated into the Gaelic clan, he understood the importance of his Masses as the indigenous ritual of his chosen community. He told me of his pride in his Cúil Aodh Mass when I met him for the last time, on 19th August 1971. He pressed a copy of the Mass into my hands as a parting gift with a reminder that I should be hearing from him on my birthday, October 4th.

Treasa O'Driscoll

Garech de Brún's telegram bearing the news of his death arrived on the morning of that very day. He also promised that friends of his would be coming through Toronto as so they did, one by one, during the months following his death when we could commiserate with one another in the loss of our beloved Sean.

Seán Ó Riada succeeded in putting art into life. He exuded a reverence for natural wisdom and a joy in the human presence. He taught me that learning is an end in itself. A greater understanding of the life that animates us all might be brought about through an intensive probing into the spirit of Seán Ó Riada and the reason for this spirit's having manifested itself at a particular time in the history of Ireland.

Some fifteen years after the death of his father, Peadar, Seán's eldest son and also a composer, came to stay with us in Toronto, ostensibly to join with me and American composer Steven Scotti in a series of performances. The outcome of that six weeks sojourn was that my two older sons Briain and Robert developed a great admiration for Peadar who began to instruct them in the art of Bodhrán (Irish drum) making. He led them on the successful mission of finding goat skins and sheep urine in the city of Toronto, all the while holding them in thrall with his accounts of life in wondrous Cúil Aodh. He became such a mentor during this period that Briain chose to journey to West Cork, attaching himself to Peadar as apprentice and neophyte. In the course of his two years spent in the Ó Riada household, Briain became a member of the men's choir which Seán had formed for the singing of his masses, and perfected his technique on the traditional flute. As a gifted teacher of music and metaphysics, Peadar made a deep and lasting impression on both my sons.

...Ó Riada did St. Patrick's work,
making masses for the people
that the spirit would touch their souls
more directly,
with notes more telling than words,
chords that were prayers...
I'm sure the old voices had warned him
that the battles would be fought in the soul
the voices of the ancestors
were always clear to him,
the communication liquid crystal,
the kind that gleams within.

the wireless of his harpsichord
was his direct link to the other side,
and being a true representative
of the silent hierarchy,
he knew that the only weapon a man has
in the realm of the unseen
is his art.

From Robert O'Driscoll, Jr.

I am a part of all that I have
Met;
Yet all experience is an arch
Wherethro'
Gleams that unraveled world...
...come, my friends,
Tis not too late to seek a
newer world.
Ulysses

Seven

FLAMES OF THE ETERNAL

The appearance of a new teacher in my life has always ignited flames of inspiration, enthusiasm and devotion. To be a true teacher is to inspire love in all who would learn from us. Love is always active in encounters which bring about a deepening of understanding in my life.

We are members of a civilization that continues to lead us into war and into attitudes that are antithetical to peace. At some level each one of us is seeking to be released from this network of fear. We need concepts that will lead us towards new beginnings and a culture that reflects our divine origins and aspirations. There are certain people I have met such as Sean Ó Riada whose personal interests have become totally aligned with the interests of their communities, people who plant seeds of renewal in the social order. They appear to work with time for the sake of the eternal and whatever exists of a corresponding ideal in me is easily drawn into the service of their cause. Visionary purpose can awaken my own responsibility for positive action especially in the artistic sphere.

In his deeply moving final work Nomos No. 2, Seán Ó Riada presented a brilliant synthesis of the European classical tradition and signaled its demise. He balked, to his own distress, at the prospect of himself setting the new and vibrant tone, for which his gift had prepared him but not his lifestyle. He demonstrated his dedication to the spirit of the times by establishing a community that would endure beyond his own lifetime, by restoring Irish traditional music to the popular consciousness of the people, and by the fusion he effected of traditional and classical musical idioms. All this he achieved in spite of his human imperfections.

At no point of our lives are we completely ready to make the perfect gesture. It must be made in spite of our imperfections, and with the humility that entails. The men I will introduce in this chapter have enriched my life and the lives of others by the divine fitness of their vision and by their willingness to take decisive action. I present them to you in the sequence in which they arrived. Each encounter uncovered some hitherto hidden aspiration of my own heart.

Treasa O'Driscoll

A Wider World Beckons

My first meeting with Richard Demarco took place in a lecture theatre of Toronto University's Architectural College in the late seventies. The room was plunged into darkness as a dynamic man of slight build gave voluble testimony to a display of slides, in support of his thesis that some contemporary art was beginning to resemble that of prehistoric cultures and the artifacts of the Celtic world. His radical views were vividly expressed as we feasted our eyes on these new and exciting images. Waving his arms to great effect he declared: "Our world is contaminated with too much art, and modern art cannot remain in one place long enough so as to become acceptable to future generations. There are too many art galleries, too many self styled artists concerned only with aesthetics and with buying and selling easily transportable artifacts!"

He mentioned his friends Joseph Beuys and Paul Neagu a lot and the fervor of his delivery was seasoned with hyperbole, anecdote, aphorism, paradox and charged with high voltages of energy.

It was a fascinating performance. After about two hours my husband nudged me and reminded me of another appointment. We were unobtrusively slinking out of the hall in the darkness when Demarco took a leap off the platform in our direction. "Wait, who are you and where are you going?" he demanded. "Our name is O'Driscoll and we unfortunately have another engagement..." we muttered apologetically. So began an association for my husband and myself that would gather momentum over several years.

An Italo-Scot with a devastating combination of Latin and Celtic fire, Demarco burst upon the consciousness of the art world in 1967 with his prodigious First Edinburgh Open 100 Exhibition, and thereby established his newly opened gallery as a first bastion of contemporary art in Britain. By 1973, the reviews of his endeavors were so glowing that such sentences as the following flash from the pages of newspapers: *He is Scotland's Dionysus, its Mars, its Mercury, its Vulcan, one of the great, charming, difficult, recklessly expansive, priceless visionaries of the world.*

His next mission was to draw the attention of the world to the Celtic origins of Europe, to a prehistoric culture that he always said makes the Renaissance seem *much more a sunset than a dawning*. The significance of this reawakening of interest in places of pilgrimage is that it, in Richard's opinion, puts modern people off balance causing them to revert to intuition and imagination. Demarco's inspiring philosophy, his magnetism and vitality caused my husband and I to become grist to his mill when he made his first visit to our house in Toronto, deciding there and then to make it his second home. He was making a whirlwind tour of North America to attract participants for a forthcoming Edinburgh Arts Journey. These journeys began in 1972 as part of an international Summer School for artists interested in exploring Scotland's Celtic roots. Gradually broadening in concept, they took the form of annual pilgrimages or rites of Summer. By 1976 it was an odyssey of seven thousand five hundred miles, a sixty-three day expedition in which he led participants over water and land, exploring hills and rivers, underground caverns associated with legend and folklore from Malta to Sardinia, Italy, Yugoslavia and back through Italy to France, England, Wales, Ireland and Scotland. In 1979 we arrived back in time for the Edinburgh Festival and an exhibition in Richard's gallery reflected the course of our travels. I presented poetry, songs and stories I had shared along the way, in caves or in palaces as the occasion demanded.

As the journey approximated the expression of his ideals, it became more difficult, more a financial and physical impossibility, causing Demarco to become more determined for it to continue. The act of daring inherent in luring a disparate group of people, artists, professors, housewives, joiners, to parts unknown by the power of suggestion, having given them only scant knowledge as to where they are going or as to whom they will meet, while defying all the common rubrics of travel, could not be advertised in a tourist magazine and was not for the faint-hearted. Juxtaposed with the discovery of little known artistic wonders were days of feast or famine, aborted schedules, missed connections, quarrels, reconciliations and the whole spectrum of human interactions.

The first step of the journey was a visit a few of us made with Louis Le Brocquy an Irish painter living in Southern France, and the Canadian sculptor Sorel Etrog, to the special unit of Her Majesty's Prison in Barlinnie, near Glasgow. Demarco had arranged for me to sing for a captive audience of the six, rated *most dangerous men* in Scotland, who were on that occasion surrounded by fourteen guards. Jimmie Boyle, (later released) who had, through Richard's intervention, established himself as a sculptor while serving a murder sentence, was amongst them. This unit was an experiment and it gave the inmates scope to explore their creativity, displayed in colorful Mexican-type murals and decorated cells. It was, nevertheless, a prison and when the gates closed behind us we were thankful for our own freedom and for a few weeks after we were not inclined to complain about anything!

For our second journey Demarco had managed to procure, skillful crew and all, the three-masted sailing ship Marques, better known to BBC viewers as Darwin's Beagle. Putting artists instead of scientists on board, was a gesture of defiance against the misapplication of survival of the fittest theory to human beings. The ultimate aspiration of human evolution is free self-actualized individuality, not to be confused with determinative collective patterns that characterize animal behavior and the less conscious aspects of human nature.

The ship was an important instrument of the periphery, giving the participants as voyagers a feeling of unity and the heightened experience of approaching sites by sea. In this vessel, we encompassed the Celtic world, tracing the route of Tristan and Iseult to the Scilly Islands and Brittany, in a final dramatic moment, discovering Carnac by moonlight. Demarco's approach to pilgrimage is in accord with Irish monastic tradition, the emphasis of which, Joseph Campbell says is *on the mystical side, not on the importance of historic events that may or may not have taken place but on the requirement that something should happen here and now in one's mind and will.* The journey awakened a true appreciation for the beauty of landscape in me, for the joy of human companionship and the music of what happens. I also discovered the importance of location in relation to art. The work of an artist, seen in the context of his studio and chosen landscape appeared as a totally natural expression of his being.

Richard Demarco with whom I remain in contact, has left a lasting impression upon me and I would like to travel

Treasa O'Driscoll

with him again. He is a man who believes that anything worthwhile can only be achieved through dialogue. My children still remember the excitement that surrounded his visits to our home and the interest in the visual arts that was sparked accordingly. He talked all the time of people he had known, people he admired, people he hoped to work with. As catalyst extraordinaire, he once declared "My part is in scouting, discovering people and places everywhere I go that are vital and inspiring and then making connections." Ever since meeting Richard I have been inspired to do likewise and I have always counted myself as one of his vast undercover army of explorers.

Between Worlds

The death of hunger striker Bobby Sands in a Belfast prison in the early eighties brought the Toronto Irish, some eight hundred strong, together to commemorate this landmark event in Irish history. I was asked to sing the Seán Ó Riada Mass at this gathering in a large auditorium. The poet John Montague was present, reciting a poem extemporaneously penned, during the ceremony. After it was over, a friend approached, inviting us to dine with her at her home on Toronto island the following evening. As we made our crossing on the ferry next day, a dark haired man slightly younger than myself, striking and intense, approached us: "Hi, I'm Alexander Blair-Ewart and I think we are all going to the same dinner party." I told him I was Irish, noting his own British accent. When I responded to his inquiry about precisely where in Ireland I was born, he said, "Ah yes, Tuam County Galway. I know it well. I lived only seven miles from there between the age of seven and fourteen." He later astounded me by his vivid recall of every hill and tree, the names and characteristics of neighbors

Stars Above the Road

and by his facility in reciting a passage in the Irish language from a text book we had both studied in national school. During the meal I overheard him and John Montague refer to the work of Rudolf Steiner whose name I was hearing for the first time. I was intrigued by their terms of reference, words hitherto unknown to me such as *etheric* and *astral*, made my heart leap.

Not long after this meeting Bob and I joined Alexander's study group, delving into *Occult Science*, one of Steiner's basic texts relating to the evolution of our earth. The comprehensive perspective of Steiner's world view gave my life a context through which to understand the twists and turns of my own biography and the mystery and purpose of life itself.

Alexander was a frequent visitor to our house, patiently revealing to us the secrets of existence that had unfolded for him in his lifelong independent spiritual research. Conversations with him informed me in a way that books to that point, had not. I loved to listen to him talk and every question I asked was given serious consideration. Bob was in the process of forming the *Centre for Celtic Studies* at the university of Toronto at the time and Alex who was Scottish often reflected on the importance of upholding the Celtic approach to life. He was succinct on the origin and distinction of the Celt, it seemed to imply a sacred calling for him:

"The Celt is an original European who has never excelled at most of the things for which European civilization is renowned: the evolution of the State, political and economic refinement, and organized religion. In the beginning of Celtic racial life, its collective spirit was a dominant force in

Europe, with druidic mystery schools at the core of its existence."

Because the druids had received a lot of bad press, regarded as they were as enemies of Christianity I wondered what direction these mystery schools might have taken.

"Christianity made its first converts in the Celtic world from among their spiritual leaders, the druids. For the other, less evolved groups this was not the case, and a pre-Christian Druidism persisted in a waning form for many centuries."

"You mean the Druids exerted a positive force in the spread of Christianity?" I was surprised by this unorthodox slant on history.

"Yes," Alex continued, "through the advanced Christian Druids, the esoteric Celtic Christian Brotherhoods sprang to life, and the whole inner force of the Celtic people became guided by this mystical Christianity."

"Did this have any connection with the monastic tradition?" I asked him.

"Many of the druidic initiates withdrew from folk life in order to complete the profound transformation that was taking place in their souls. Several monastic streams were established to facilitate the higher embodiment of Christianity, a spiritual path that transcends all racial and national barriers."

"Celtic Christian initiates were wholly committed to acknowledging the living presence of Christ in every moment. This inspired the inner vitality of later Irish missionaries so that they could revitalize the religious life of Europe."

"What happened to the pagan druidic stream?" I wondered.

"It fell into the obscurity of regional tribal life for the followers who had not been converted to Christianity. These pagan societies formed into witchcraft cults, still in existence but in a completely degenerate form."

"I suppose one could say that the Celtic roots are as rich and firmly entrenched as is the ancient Judaic root in Christianity?"

"The esoteric spirituality practiced by our Celtic forebears is an undying light in the world. There has never been anything compulsory or mandatory about this form of Christianity that is mindful of the action of love in culture. A great light shines in Celtic poetry, language, music, a rich mystical dimension."

"The term Celt is rather loosely used and is open to many definitions," I remarked.

Alexander responded passionately: "The Celtic revival demands that we know in contemporary terms what a Celt is. If a people are to be defined by the best that is embodied in them, then the definition of a Celt would be – an esoteric Christian. Because Celtic culture presented an alternative to the civilization of its times, its revival could be taken as an indication that the spiritual life of the West is about to be revitalized. In the same way that the early missionaries recognized no social or cultural barriers in their resolve to uplift the spiritual life of Europe, so esoteric Christianity must address itself to the total spectrum of life, particularly in North America, where the Celtic revival seems to be gathering momentum."

Alexander gave me the first book of my extensive Steiner collection. Entitled *Christianity As Mystical Fact.* He explained, when he took it from his pocket to give to me during our first long talk:

Treasa O'Driscoll

"This book is the first of a series of spiritual teachings which makes clear the path followed by our Celtic mystical ancestors, but presented in a way which is intelligible to twentieth century man. For a true esotericism is never merely the preservation of arcane traditions and ritual forms but the constant rebirth of humanity's spiritual heart."

A Music of the Spheres

Christopher Bamford of Lindisfarne Press called me in the Autumn of 1984 to ask if I would help raise funds for the publication of a book by a Hungarian musician/chemist named Georg Kühlewind. The book was being translated from the German and would be entitled *Becoming Aware of the Logos*. I remember spending the Christmas period of that year transfixed by this profound meditation on the prologue to the Gospel of St. John. Every line was ground for contemplation arising out of a true creative thinking of the heart. When I had the honor of meeting Dr. Kühlewind a year later, he told me that while he was writing the book he experienced himself as overshadowed by the spirit of John.

In March of 1985, I received a call from a pianist of my acquaintance asking if he could introduce me to a Yugoslavian violinist. Within half an hour I was opening my door to Miha Pogacnik and to a new chapter in my life. No sooner was he seated in my living room than he came straight to the point:

"I wanted to meet you because I sensed as soon as I heard your name that you were the person who should represent IDRIART in Toronto."

"What," I queried, "is IDRIART?"

"IDRIART," he replied, "is that which is not yet."

I liked him instantly because I knew he spoke my language! What he had to say sounded strangely familiar although he was bringing me news of a revolutionary movement in the arts that had been officially named **I**nstitut pour le **D**evelopment des **R**elations **I**nterculturelles par l'**ART**. He told me that he became director of the Chartres Summer Festival in 1981, when the famous Cathedral was used for the first time in recent history for the performance of music. By 1983, the annual festival was attracting up to two thousand people from thirty-five countries. Out of this event a vital concept in the performance and appreciation of the arts arose. People inspired at Chartres, carried on the initiative and chapters rapidly sprang up in over twenty countries where Miha inaugurated arts festivals prepared by volunteers. Pogacnik believed in breaking through cocoons of money and elitism, realizing that a well dressed affluent audience is not necessarily God's gift to the artist. From a young age Miha determined to devote himself to educating audiences so that the experience of the listener might more closely match his own informed, concentrated attention as a player. The artists who rally to his call, many of them celebrities, proclaim their performing experience at IDRIART festivals to be highlights in their efforts to truly communicate with an audience. I reminded Miha of a statement of Gogol which seemed relevant to his aspirations: "If art does not accomplish the miracle of transforming the soul of the spectator it is not fulfilling its mission in the world."

Miha responded: "I am in total agreement with that! We have set ourselves the goal to work in such a way, that everybody participates inwardly so intensely, that new vistas may open for many and not just for the players... When artists and participants take on the responsible role of performer the festival itself becomes a work of art...

lectures, artistic courses of various kinds, introductions to more active perceiving of the arts, music, drama and eurythmy are offered. Exhibitions are set up, possibilities arranged for meetings and discussions and space is left for improvised activities. Yet we try to apply musical principles to all this work..."

There was an urgency in his tone of voice when he said the following and I became aware of his deep sense of mission:

"Today the whole world is in a very dangerous and explosive state with one main problem being the isolation among peoples. Artists are called upon to take a more active social role. To use mythological language: we together with our Muses are called to serve the spirit of our time (*Zeitgeist*) who does not want to know any national boundaries. And it is only proper for the Arts and people who want to permeate themselves with them, that they move freely to any place of the world. This is unique about IDRIART festivals, our audiences move along with us to different countries. We try to organize short but strong events at specially chosen places worldwide, always ready to change, to rethink, to improvise."

His remarks reminded me of ideas I had while reading *Becoming Aware of the Logos*. But he had not mentioned any connection with Hungary and I tentatively asked:

"Does the name Georg Kühlewind mean anything to you? I have recently read a book of his that somehow has prepared me for what you are telling me..."

Miha gave a great cry of delight.

"Georg is my mentor! He and Jurgen Schrieffer are the godfathers of our movement! You will meet him at our festival in Sacramento, California if you will join us there next year."

...And so it came about.

The Red Cross of Art

My life was greatly enhanced during the seven years I spent as an active co-worker for this exciting movement. Inspired to bring people together at a time of tremendous change in the world, Pognacnik's visits to Canada brought us news of distant places where the need for social renewal was urgent. As the calls from our brothers and sisters in Central and Eastern Europe, in Russia, South America and Tibet reached our chapters, IDRIART began to be acknowledged as the Red Cross of Art. Miha's concerts were punctuated with exhortations. He urged us to travel with him. In a letter to co-workers in 1991 he wrote: "It is incredible what is wanted and needed in the USSR and Central Europe.... The greatest need of people everywhere is to meet you, to talk to you, to know you and to work together with you... Please do come. Your active participation is the core of IDRIART."

Violinist Victor Costanzi and his harpist wife, Rita were Miha's representatives in Western Canada. As leading musicians they played a vital role in the artistic life of Vancouver. They invited me to visit them in 1990 and interrupted their busy concert schedule to organize a concert for me. The warmth of their welcome, the ambience of the city, the fact that my children could be enrolled at the Waldorf High School all contributed to my decision to move to Vancouver. My fruitful collaboration with the Costanzis paved the way for more visits by Miha and his associates to Canada.

Treasa O'Driscoll

The tenth anniversary of the founding of IDRIART occurred in 1991. A major festival was held in Chartres Cathedral which I attended along with other Canadians. One thousand participants were drawn from the some thirty-five countries in which IDRIART was by then established.

Chartres stands most complete, architecturally and iconographically of all the great Gothic cathedrals of the world. A monument to human striving, love and devotion, its site Celtic in origin, constituting geometry in space and musical in all its aspects. Chartres has become, in the words of August Rodin "a hymn of praise for eternity... When faced with a marvel... the sublime summary of centuries... one is hushed by an admiration that surpasses words." It was this hush which set the tone for E. Peppings (1901-1981) St. Matthews Passion, one of the most remarkable choral works of the 20th century, performed by a choir schooled in the method of Werbeck singing and conducted by their teacher Jurgen Schrieffer.

The unearthly purity of this work roused even the bats, who flew noiselessly above in their own paean of praise. This singing involves the cultivation of inner hearing and releases therapeutic forces, which on this occasion were powerfully experienced by the listeners. Participants in the choir were drawn from many walks of life as indeed were the builders of Chartres Cathedral, amongst whom were those who chanted, as they hauled huge stones from quarries some five kilometers away.

George Kühlewind's inspiring talk at Chartres arose out of the spirit of the moment and I shall share a brief aspect of it from notes I took at the time.

"Attention is the natural prayer which we perform towards the truth that is living in us, to bring it to show itself. Our power of attentiveness is our sacred power force but it is threatened from many sides. It has the possibility of growing more and more autonomous. If attention is concentrated on a theme it has the power of changing from grasping to opening. If attentiveness is empty, then something can fill it from above."

Jurgen Schrieffer told us about the way in which we can experience the message of Christ in music. Beethoven's 9th symphony he said, expresses a reminder to us that we stand alone and that a group soul can no longer support us. Mozart who has been called 'beloved of God' conveys, in the music of *Magic Flute*, how necessary it is to walk the inner path of freedom.

My most abiding memory of the festival was of a rather unusual outing, which had a peculiar druidic fitness about it. An excursion was planned whereby hundreds of people set out in the dead of night from Chartres, in a convoy of buses and cars, led pied-piper-like by Miha Pogacnik, the strains of whose violin, lured us on. In the gathering dawn, I could barely discern a large Celtic dolmen upon which Miha admonished me to stand. With feet firmly placed on this stony altar of time, I felt empowered to speak and sing sounds appropriate to the occasion, while hundreds stood with their backs to me, our faces now raised in homage to the rising sun. Gongs began to sound, their diminishing tones drawing us with them into meditative silence. It was a beautiful Sunday morning; with open hearts and happy faces we formed a circle, and quietly ate the abundance of good croissants and hot coffee, which seemed to appear out of nowhere. Then Miha played again. I sang all the way back to the car, field after field of glorious sunflowers lighting our way. I remembered more words of Pogacnik's: "Every landscape on this earth carries within itself a memory and its own story that seeks to reveal itself to humankind and in that way to contribute to the diversity of human society."

Into The Deep Heart's Core
>And the spark behind fear
>recognized as life, leaps
>into flame....
>>From David Whyte

My involvement with the work of Dr. Ross Laing who ranks, in my opinion, as a significant western Master and teacher of perennial wisdom, deserves a book in itself. A member of his core group from 1988 to 1990, I sat in the circle with him almost daily and learned through direct experience how to identify underlying patterns in human behavior that interfere with our fundamental desire, to love and be loved by one another.

Ross chooses to describe himself as a metaphysician in the Socratic mode and a radical psychiatrist in the Claude Steiner mode. *The Toronto Institute of Self Healing* became the context for a new style of encounter he introduces to a growing number of people seeking to become more genuine in their relationships. It was my privilege to engage with Dr. Laing in the first wave of this experiment through which I experienced fundamental life changes and profound psychological healing. In his approach, self healing is defined as *becoming the true self*. His genius was to make people realize that the manner in which they thought, felt, and acted brought about their actual state of being. People could enter deeply into the present moment and begin to throw off the burdens of the past in the environment of safety and acceptance Ross could provide.

In our current climate of specialization, clear lines are drawn between professions and it is rare to encounter a doctor who embodies and fulfills the originally integrated functions of physician/priest/philosopher. Laing presents a paradigm of wholeness that promotes a healthy functioning at physical, emotional and spiritual levels of being. He said once, "What we are working with here is consciousness, seeking to transform it from the state in which we find it."

His stated aim is to comfort the afflicted and afflict the comfortable and my experience of his therapy included both these modalities. Ross offered me and others the opportunity to observe how remote our habitual behavior was from what we wishfully imagined it to be, how far removed we were in the actual living of our lives from the ideals we espoused. He reminded us that Aldous Huxley was on the right track when he wrote:

If only I knew who in fact I am, I should cease to behave as what I think I am. If I stopped behaving as what I think I am, I should know who I am.

Acquiring a whole new set of concepts from the New Age smorgasbord will not of itself guarantee a fundamental change in behavior. A close friend, Anne Stockton once remarked to me, "Ideas do a stimulating dance in the middle of our space. But do they travel horizontally in one ear and out the other? What trickles down into the heart? How much drips down into the will?"

The symptoms of distress in evidence in our lives belong to a culture we all help to shape. The antidote must also arise out of that social context I believe. The one-on-one relationship between therapist and client is but one aspect of a more comprehensive group process. Any disfunction in social interaction can be identified and healed in a safe and therapeutic environment.

Those who sought Dr. Laing out were suffering from contraction in the soul life, in flight from circumstances that brought hidden fears to the surface of consciousness; fear of failure, fear of success, fear of violence, fear of intimacy, fear of life. The variations on the theme were endless although we might not have been able to identify their common source. Ross, through vigorous discipline and witnessing, had already found the depths of love within himself to lead us into an open-eyed encounter with the autonomous force of fear itself. This truly was my entry into what Yeats had termed *the foul rag and bone shop of the heart*. Another revered friend Robert Sardello had made his own brave entry into the fray with the publication of his book *Freeing The Soul From Fear*. He said of fear in his introduction:

> *Besides showing up as individual psychological difficulties, we now have to contend with this destructive force as a cultural phenomenon that touches us all more deeply and significantly than we might ever imagine. The soul life of humanity is in danger...*

Ross developed four basic principles, which today are fundamental to my life and which I continue to share with others.

Deep Diaphragmatic Breathing: To breath in such a way that the waist expands to its maximum at each breath for twenty minutes twice a day.

Affirmation: As we began each conscious breathing session Ross encouraged us to repeat the following words:

"I am willing to experience and express the fullness of my feelings and thoughts in ways that uplift me and all creation."

Stroking: We were frequently reminded to express self appreciation, self-acknowledgment and unconditionally loving compassion, to foster a spirit of gratitude and celebration, to engage in physical stroking that would create a sensation of warmth in the heart.

Responsibility: We had to present a willingness to explore the concept of taking full responsibility for creating the quality of our own experience.

Ross devised these guidelines while holding steady to his goal of thirty years. He had witnessed his beloved brother die at the age of twenty of Hodgkins disease. He resolved then to devote himself to finding the cause of and antidote to the cancerous condition. He became convinced that our way of breathing is crucial to our health and well being. He could also prove that the inner picture we carry of ourselves, positive or negative, influences our state of bodily health and our quality of life. He had once been a shy, awkward and relatively anti-social person himself. "Nobody could empty a room faster than I could."

As we sat contentedly in his peaceful, loving and magnetic presence we could hardly believe this to be true but it helped us to realize that we too might create an environment to accord with our inner aspirations. "The more you visualize the qualities you aim towards the more form will follow. There are contrary influences, dependencies, but they do not determine the outcome!" we were told.

Becoming Free

The greater the difficulties the greater the potential for good contained in them. I sought refuge at the Institute when I could no longer cope with the daily circumstances of my life...

I have already alluded to the manic depressive disorder that became entrenched in my husband. This naturally caused great upheaval in our household and resulted in his periodic suspension from university teaching. The family became used to a survival mode that functioned in reaction to the *enfant terrible* in our midst, all attempts to establish a routine were confounded, even the distinction between day and night became blurred for me when a manic phase took hold. My social life dwindled to nothing and most of our friends dropped away, with the notable exception of Bill Graham (now Canada's minister for Defence) and his remarkable wife Cathy, the generosity of whose spirit, the practicality of whose assistance has left our family forever in their debt. I was torn between a need to protect the children and compassion for Bob, in whom this syndrome had taken root after the near-fatal car accident, years before. Having myself been relegated to the position of enemy in his bizarre order of things, I had to accept that there was no further hope for communication with the person with whom I had shared so much. Yet I hesitated to take the step of leaving with the children, afraid of the battle that might ensue...

I remember Dr. Laing's first question:

"Why are you here?"

"I am here because I can no longer cope with my husband's paranoia."

"You cannot cope with your paranoia." he responded.

"You misunderstand me, Dr. Laing. I am speaking about my husband's paranoia."

"Your husband is your mirror," he gently replied.

My cry of dismay at the shock of this possibility was my first introduction to the notion that my own inner state might be somehow reflected in the external conditions of my life. I was unaware as yet, that the numbness I experienced in my physical body was due to the grip that fear had on me at a cellular level. This manifested in my environment as severe emotional disturbance always claiming my attention. There were daily revelations after that about the underlying patterns in attitude and behavior that led me to experience these circumstances. I learned about my own neurosis by watching and assisting other group members in their processing of similar material and through Ross' intuitive interventions. All my life I had been excessively tolerant of unwelcome behavior, hungry for approval. I had avoided confronting issues out of fear of reprisal and was always more than willing to compromise my own wishes.

The only curriculum at this academy was life itself and our homework entailed a willingness to deal with issues that arose on the home front. I found that it was much easier to be strong and to hold one's ground when supported by a trusted community. Every direction given to me by Ross was intuitively right and guaranteed to empower me. He noticed, for instance, that I could hardly utter one sentence without mentioning the name of my husband with whom I was excessively preoccupied. He asked me to count the number of these references made in the course of the day. I had to continue to report on this in nightly phone calls to him until I had entirely broken the habit. Habits do not evaporate of themselves but we can outwit them if we adopt the right strategy. The energy that is thereby released can be channeled into more positive action.

After two years of attendance at the Institute, I had succeeded in breaking free of my own entanglement with Bob's behavior, which remained unaltered. Only I had changed, and could now remove myself from the situation. Ross' definition of the guilt that had dogged me, "The impulse to change being turned back against oneself," had helped to free me of it.

I had a new and practical goal to live up to—the aspiration to maintain an open heart regardless of circumstances. Nor did I harbor any more illusions that I could help anybody who had not specifically asked for help.

The emphasis on our group work was not so much on what we would talk about, but on how we spoke to one another. Ross operated on the premise that ninety four percent of the unspoken in our communication can be gleaned from the tone of our voices. When we really listen we become aware that most people speak out of a tone of desperation, he said, and this is due to the fact that we were never truly loved for our own sake.

I was often stopped in mid-sentence: "Are you aware of your tone?"

In listening to others we were encouraged to hear what was going on behind the words and to respond accordingly, thus establishing more of a feeling connection with the other.

We learned to question one another without resorting to accusations, never starting with "You should..." or "You always..." or "You did not..."

Ross also expressed the wish to "clear the world of gossip." This impressed me particularly, as one of a race, about which G.K. Chesterton said—'The Irish are a fair people. They never speak well of one another!'

We agreed to only speak well of one another in absence but to be very direct with our hidden judgments in the context of the group.

When criticism was leveled in its proper context and resolved there and then, it curbed our tendency towards backbiting. A decision not to speak about anything that transpired in the group, increased the energetic momentum and ensured the integrity of our whole endeavor.

I resorted often to poetry in the course of this process and I spontaneously recited at moments when we were all at a loss for words. One of my favorites was by R.D. Laing. A namesake and mentor for Ross, this maverick Scottish psychiatrist had based his research on the observation that we do not experience each other's experience, *only* each other's behavior...

> There is something I don't know
> that I'm supposed to know,
> I don't know what it is I don't know,
> And yet am supposed to know,
> And I feel I look stupid
> if I seem both not to know it
> And not know what is I don't know.
> Therefore I pretend I know it...
>
> From R.D. Laing, Knots

What happened at the Institute constituted *the only show in town* for a period of time. There I could observe and participate in an unfolding, never-ending human drama. I witnessed scenes of apparent conflict and saw them move towards resolution. I noticed the scapegoating which is such a part of all group interaction, was laid to rest as families were restored to the fundamental vibration of love that bound them in the first place. Family members flew in from far-flung places when a moment of reconciliation was at hand. Such joyful reunions confirmed my belief in the power of love. I often lay on the carpet and listened to Ross interact with new arrivals. One day, a couple in their twenties presented their story. They had fallen in love with each other and had decided to live together, only there was a snag—the young man already had a wife. What should they do? Ross's first question was addressed to the girl.

"Have you spoken to your sister?"

"I don't have a sister," came her reply.

He repeated the question twice until she realized that the *sister* he had in mind was the woman whose husband she desired. Ross then suggested that *she* attend their next session because *she* too was a vital player in whatever would enfold. In listening to such exchanges I was always tuning into that-which-is-not-yet, becoming acquainted with the *Presence* in another of its guises. Many things spoken by Ross are forever etched in memory.

> *"Healing is perfectly natural. The only reason we don't know about this is that we work against it twenty-four hours of the day. You don't have to do anything except breathe with the diaphragm and be willing to experience the fullness of feeling."*
>
> *"You must demonstrate your ability to keep your word no matter what."*
>
> *"Unconditional love is the practice of unconditionally living on the creative edge."*

"Unless information is embodied it has no chance of generation."
Ross Laing

Eight

UNDERSTANDING THE MYSTERY

The separation from my husband brought my involvement with university affairs to an end. I was no longer privy to detailed reports on the progress of the Celtic Studies program, no longer exposed to the latest scholarship in the field. What I had learned would not be forgotten but the academic relevance of the subject matter would have to be adapted to fit the now more compelling context of a conscious spiritual path. My years of independent study of esoteric traditions had made me eager to apply the principles I had gleaned and my experience at the *Institute of Self Healing* was a practical step in that direction. I had been reminded time and time again that every ending implied a beginning on another level. The recurring motif of the spiral image in Celtic art conveyed this universal truth very directly, *in our end is our beginning.*

This new beginning was a time of spiritual awakening for me.

The mystery of the passion, death and resurrection of Christ Jesus, as the pivotal cosmic event of human history continued to influence me deeply. The prolific writing of Rudolf Steiner about this turning point in evolution provided a comprehensive context for the study of *The New Testament* and the *Gospel of St. John* in particular. Meaning, not religious fervor, was my motivation and I sought everywhere for the deepening understanding of this mystery. I found its resonance in several contemporary writings as well. The mission and deed of Christ as the *reality in which we live*, will of the necessity of its nature, constantly reveal itself to human beings. It finds expression in a multitude of ways ranging from fundamental to refined.

I was introduced to James Redfield by his sister Joy, a close friend of mine, and quickly realized I was in the presence of a remarkable individual whose mystic realization over twenty years before had led to his writing *The Celestine Prophecy*. Redfield reveals the ministry of Christ as one of selfless service, inexorably determining the destiny and redemption of every human soul.

> *He knew he was here to bring a new energy into the world, a new culture based on love. His message was this: the one God was a holy spirit, a divine energy, whose existence could be felt and proven experientially. Coming into spiritual awareness meant more than rituals and sacrifices and public prayer. It involved repentance that was an inner psychological shift based on a suspension of the ego's addictions, a transcendental "letting go"...*

The spiral of birth and death also finds representation in Redfield's *The Tenth Insight*. The characters in this book become aware that each one enters the world with an original *birth vision* with which a vision of an after life is juxtaposed.

...we all have an original intention that is positive...our responsibility is to hold the ideal for everyone we meet. That's the true interpersonal ethic; that's how we uplift, that's the contagion of the new awareness that is encircling the planet. We either fear that human culture is falling apart or we can hold the vision that we are awakening. Either way our expectation is a prayer that goes out as a force that tends to bring about the end we envision. Each of us can choose between these two futures...

The Importance of Meaning

The Logos has entered the invisibility of the human heart, and in this way *the true light has entered the true temple. (Georg* Kühlewind) It is in the eternal exchange of love between human beings that the Christ truly lives.

One of the most loving recommendations made by Jesus is; *let not your hearts be troubled.* What often troubles the heart is an absence of meaning. The soul is nurtured in the knowledge that we live in a world that is full of meaning, everything in nature and in the innate spiritual make-up of humanity is an expression of cosmic speech. There is a longing in human hearts to be able to hear the *symphony of the created word*, the notes which also sound in us because we ourselves are its instruments. Human speech has the possibility of conveying purity of sound and meaning. Words have both an outer and an inner meaning and we can recover some of the lost significance of a word such as *disaster* for instance. Its fundamental meaning is *adrift from the stars*, from the larger cosmic context we inhabit. If we use words without being aware of their broader connotations we speak in abstractions remote from the heart of things.

A story from the Gospel of St Luke demonstrates how the actual speaking of Christ Jesus could penetrate the hearts of the disciples with understanding. This gift of deliberate and expressive speech was bestowed upon the apostles at Pentecost and remains available to all sincere human beings. Two disciples were walking the road to Emmaus on the day referred to thereafter as Easter Sunday. They were talking together earnestly about the extraordinary events that had recently taken place in Palestine. Jesus himself appeared and joined them but they did not recognize his features.

He asked, "What are you discussing?"

They told him of the teaching mission of the man they knew as Jesus, his travels, condemnation, and crucifixion, remarking in surprise. "Are you the only one who does not know?"

They related how some women of their acquaintance had gone to the tomb that morning and had seen a vision of angels where the body of Jesus had lain. The stranger who was the Risen Christ explained to them why it was necessary for events to unfold as they did, interpreting the scriptures to indicate that all had been fulfilled as written. When they stopped for the night He accompanied them to the resting place. It was only when He broke bread that they recognized Him.

They said afterwards: *"Did not our hearts burn within us when He talked to us on the road, when he opened up the scriptures to us!"*

For such a response to be called forth in them implies that they ceased to be believers as such or onlookers, but that they themselves were brought wholeheartedly into the experiences that were being described. Here was truth not gauged in terms of right and wrong but rather uncovered.

> All truths wait in all things
> They neither hasten their own
> Delivery nor resist it...
> From Walt Whitman

Christ gave us his gifts of Grace and Truth as recorded in the Gospel of St. John, as the ground of a heavenly order that would free us from the Old Testament law, fulfilled by His deed and superceded by his new law of Love. The one commandment that Jesus emphasized was, *That you love one another as I have loved you*, an evolved synthesis of all the previous commandments conveyed through Moses. It implies that we love others for their own sakes. To live by this commandment is to align completely with the earthly mission of esoteric Christianity, making the central purpose of one's life, a coming to birth of the spirit. Meister Eckhart has described the signs that enable us to know when this birth has occurred in the soul.

> *Once this birth has really occurred, no creatures can hinder you; instead they will all direct you to God and his birth. Take lightning as an analogy. Whatever it strikes, whether tree, beast or man, it turns at once towards itself... All things become simply God to you, for in all things you notice only God, just as a man who stares long at the sun sees the sun in whatever he afterwards looks at. If this is lacking, this looking for and seeking God in all and sundry, then you lack this birth...*
> From Meister Eckhart.

Soul Symbols

The emblem that serves as a reminder to each carrier of this impulse towards rebirth is the Sword of Light borne by the mythological Lugh, the Celtic Sun-God before whom the servants of darkness scattered like chaff before the wind. It is also reminiscent of the sword brandished by Michael, the ruling archangel of our epoch. Symbolically it is also the invisible weapon borne by every *Knight of the Word*.

Visualize yourself holding this gleaming instrument of light between solar plexus and third eye, whenever you are called upon to speak words of truth. It is a double-edged sword because it cuts through illusion and falsehood in oneself and one's surroundings.

Of equal importance on the path of soul is the Celtic Cross, such a familiar feature of the Irish landscape. When we view our lives from perspectives of both outer and inner development we create the symbol of a cross. The horizontal line stretches from birth to death and represents our story in time and historical context. The vertical line represents the Heaven/Earth axis that informs every moment of life but of which we are not always consciously aware. Around their intersecting lines a circle of wholeness can appear.

The points that make up the circumference of the circle represent the aspect of oneself that is mirrored back in every encounter with another person. This *circle of friends* hovers over my heart and holds the secret of who I am. The entire cross represents the balance point I achieve when I fully accept the conditions of earthly life, mindful of the Heavenly order that permeates existence and of the blessings inherent in my conscious attention to material things.

When life is regulated in accordance with spiritual insight into the mission of Christ we can no longer take our own presence in the world for granted. *Our embodied presence is seen to be not so much miraculous as stupendous in import*, stated Rudolf Steiner.

When we live in mindfulness of divine presence, constantly aware that we are being renewed by this grail substance of which the mythological Celtic grail the *cauldron of plenty* was a prefiguration, we avoid a hardening of the heart. We also avoid the premature hardening of arteries, that comes about when mechanical memory holds sway. This lamentable condition was described by Yeats.

> ...We have fed the heart on fantasies,
> The hearts grown brutal from
> the fare
> More substance in our enmities
> Than in our love...
>   From WB Yeats, The Stare's Nest by my Window

The word *Grail* implies gradual (grail–gradalis–gradual) leading from dullness to doubt to final spiritual enlightenment, the path of many contemporary Parcivals. Joseph Campbell called the Grail legend, *the founding myth of Western civilization.* He spoke about it when he came to Toronto in 1978 to open the *Festival of Celtic Consciousness.* The importance of this myth lies in the fact that the path trodden by Parcival is an archetypal one with which we can all identify and that it leads the soul to an experience of Christ himself, as described by Christian Morgenstern:

> I have seen man in his foremost
> formation
> I know the universe in its
> foundation.
> I know that love, love is
> its utmost aim
> And that to love, love more
> And more I came
> My arms, as He has done,
> I open wide
> Like Him, I'd like to hold
> The world inside…

Joseph of Arimethea is believed to have gathered up the last drops of blood that issued from the wounds of the crucified Christ into a chalice that had been fashioned out of an emerald that had once fallen to earth – a stone from the crown of Lucifer. The human blood stream is now the container of this precious etherized blood stream which once mingled with the earth, thus we are now called upon to become ourselves, chalices of the Grail. Several years ago an image came to me in meditation. I saw a chalice standing on a crescent moon and a flower rose out of the cup to receive as it were, a sunbeam of love.

I regard the moon as representative of the unconscious conditioning of earthly life that has to be transformed and out of which a grail cup is formed from which the flower that is our own unique spirit can emerge. In a lecture Rudolf Steiner gave in March of 1909, he referred to the fact that Parzival was a collective name amongst the pupils of Titurel, in England, in the following revelation:

> *In the deep solitude of the mountains, in which he stood, Parzival directed his sight to the infinite depth below him, looked in front and back of himself, to the right and left, into the infinite distances, and an indescribable feeling of reverence and devotion came over him, for the divinity which revealed itself in everything. He felt the great oneness of all. And he addressed this prayer to Him: 'You great All, to whom I feel above, below and next to me, who is everywhere, whether I look forward or backward, I want to surrender myself to you, merge my self into you.'*

St. Patrick had a corresponding revelation which composed his *breastplate*. When he recited it he became invisible to any enemy who was lurking about. It is a wonderful prayer of protection and a reminder to me of the healing presence which enfolds us.

Stars Above the Road

Christ with me
Christ before me
Christ behind me
Christ in me
Christ over me
Christ to my right
Christ to my left
Christ where I rise
Christ where I sit
Christ where I lie
Christ where I stand
Christ in the heart of everyone
who thinks of me
Christ in the mouth of
everyone who speaks of me

A choral version of the breastplate entitled *The Deer's Cry*, has been superbly arranged by Irish composer Shaun Davey. I had the privilege of being the soloist in this piece when it was performed in concert by the choir of *The Chalice Of Repose Project* conducted by Therese Schroeder-Sheker, May 2000, in Missoula, Montana. The timeless relevance of Patrick's words were received in hushed and reverent silence by a large audience.

The Parcival of William Von Eschenbach's story had a dreamy consciousness of love before he experienced his five years of trial and suffering and it was only through the pain of self knowledge that he felt the tender calling of an overflowing love that flowed out to embrace the world. This love gave rise to the healing of his uncle the king and the surrounding kingdom, which had fallen waste. Our birth vision also emerges out of the revelation of this Love.

I was coming myself to the end of a cycle of difficulties in my life when my parents invited me to visit them in 1996. Arriving from Canada I made my way from Shannon

Treasa O'Driscoll

airport to their home in County Galway. As soon as I crossed the threshold of the modest bungalow in which I had been reared, I entered a sanctuary of peace. I sat with my mother and father around the fire each night as we recited the decades of the rosary, a tradition I had often resisted in my teenage years but which they had devotedly maintained. It allowed them to hold the lives of their seven children in an uninterrupted stream of intercessory prayer. In the silence that followed one evening I had a remarkable instance of remembering. I experienced myself being drawn inwardly into the field of unified radiation which my parents' lifelong bond of love has generated. I recognized it as the compelling force that had attracted me, and led to my conception. A resolution formed in my heart to live in total trust of this wisdom-filled direction and to allow love to awaken in me towards everyone I would thenceforth meet. For I knew that when love is present the truth is present, reality is present, creativity is present. It is said that we are on earth at this time to realize a new heaven and a new earth. The newness arises out of a co-creative endeavor between the spiritual and human worlds. Such prayers as the following further a collective infusing of the world with love and meaning:

> May the events that seek me
> come unto me;
> May I receive them with a
> quiet mind
> Through the father's *fount* of
> peace
> On which we work
>
> May the people who seek me
> Come unto me;
> May I receive them

with an understanding heart
Through the Christ's stream of love,
In which we live.
>From Adam Bittleston

Life Rhythms

A thread of underlying purpose shapes the character of the unique individuality to which every 'I' can lay claim. 'Character is destiny' according to a Chinese adage. The keepers of the thread are our angels.

Dieter Lauenstein in his book *Biblical Rhythms in Biography* tells of how the angel shows us a preview of the life to come and guides the forces that shape the embryo. The angel exerts an influence on the parents and on the wider circle of people around the child.

I had been brought up to acknowledge the presence of a guardian angel whose task it was to lead me and protect me. Surrounded as I was by loving and protecting adults I had no difficulty in accepting further evidence of divine providence in my life. This angel I was told, would facilitate a review of my life from time to time. Because amnesia had set in regarding my reason for being on earth, the angel might have to intervene occasionally to keep me on course. The intervention of the angel, I was led to believe, is not required when our lives are proceeding according to a regular and harmonious rhythm. We make our souls accessible to angelic communion during sleep, when we cultivate an attitude of generosity and gratitude during our waking hours. As a child I recited as I was bidden, the mighty prayer to my guardian angel before falling asleep. The sleep which restores spiritual momentum is essential to physical and mental health throughout our lives.

The angel draws near again in later life to give a fresh infusion of spiritual resolve. Goethe declared that while we are idealists in youth and become realists in the years of active will, we are mystics in old age. W.B. Yeats was sixty-one when he wrote:

> ...An aged man is but a paltry
> Thing,
> A tattered coat upon a stick,
> Unless
> Soul clap its hands and sing,
> And louder sing,
> For every tatter in its mortal dress
>
> From W.B. Yeats, *Sailing to Byzantium*

Dieter Lauenstein clarified his views on the deepening of the soul life:

> *Both our own efforts and those of our angel are necessary if we are indeed, to become mystics; it does not happen by itself. If no deepening of the soul life occurs, then the soul becomes distorted and slowly becomes barren. Today we see people living a lie against age. Only on a high level of the soul can we remain young without injury. At this level we should become ever childlike, precisely this enables us to become mystical in the good sense intended by Goethe.*

I have been assisting my angel along the way by conducting a backwards look over the events of my day before falling asleep at night. Beginning at the end it entails letting pictures of the day's experiences pass before my mind's eye, watching myself go through them without judgement. This helps to disengage my thinking from its accustomed habit of holding on to fixed points of view or charges of feeling. I gradually become more capable of meeting the events of life with equanimity and with less attachment to outcome. I consequently experience myself as a different person today than I was before. Rudolf Steiner remarked: *Life is our great* teacher. *If you live from erroneous assumptions, life will correct these errors and demonstrate a deeper truth.*

> *"I believe that this age, as a matter of course and consequence, will create something like a separation of single individuals from the trends of our time. Individual people will begin to think differently of themselves and will find out their own inward stirring, new ways, spiritual ways. It seems to me that for instance Goethe had a circumference of consciousness far in excess of his contemporaries of the 19th century. This was strongly upheld by Rudolf Steiner and with this I fully agree. In a certain sense atomistic science has a significance, namely in as much as it is in the hands of people who are in no way equipped for it. For the progress of mankind it has no significance. The path of progress I see is in the occupation of modern man with himself, with his inwardness, in the way indicated by Rudolf Steiner."*
> From T.S. Eliot (in an address he gave on West German radio in the 1950's)

The path of inwardness takes on a different coloration in each cycle of life. I found that as I approached middle age I became preoccupied with what have been identified as the three grail questions and I have found it useful to hold them in the background of my nightly retrospective.

a) What is the Grail? B) Whom does it serve? C) Who serves it?

I chose to rephrase these questions in a more practical form:

a) Do I have a task to perform that I love? B) Who benefits from my loving task? C) By what path of inner development is my desire to serve inspired?

Treasa O'Driscoll

> There is no fixed law, no established knowledge of God set up by
> prophets or priests, that can stand against the revelation of a life
> lived with integrity in the spirit of its own brave truth.
> *Joseph Campbell*

Nine

THE HERO WITHIN

Parzival's grail quest reveals, according to Joseph Campbell, that *there is no fixed law, no established knowledge of God set up by prophets or priests, that can stand against the revelation of a life lived with integrity in the spirit of its own brave truth*. This myth reflects the spiritual journey of each human life. The naive would-be knight that was Parzival, had to forge his own path by grace of providence. Foolish, ignorant and ungainly he set out on an adventure of trial and error, which assumed a heroic dimension because he left a trail, which can be followed up to the present day.

...take heart from the child within,
The only one who will
Recognize who you are.
Discipline your impulses

> And, by stopping, stay
> straightforward
> In the world of complexity
> When entanglement can
> obscure
> The path to the Grail.
>> Linda Sussman in Speech of the Grail

The story of Parzival turns upon an act of speech. Although he finds the castle of the Grail relatively easily he cannot formulate the question which lies within his destiny to ask. He has not yet learned to listen to what is in the hearts of others. Only after years of hardship tempered by the trials of life and through his renewal of faith on Good Friday is he afforded a second chance to enter the castle. Speaking finally out of true compassion bred of suffering, he articulates the question: *Uncle what ails thee?* A simultaneous healing of his uncle and environs occurs.

This journey into compassion is the one we are all charged to make. The grail, nurturing and enhancing according to each one's needs and capacities, nourishes the invisible web of relationships through which destiny weaves. As vessel of inspiration, the Grail makes its substance available to the receptive imagination of poets and artists and to that element in each of us AE termed *the hero within*. The *hero* is my hidden identity, a source of solid ground inside me, a kind of organic presence in me that can divine and witness and know and remain constant throughout all vicissitudes.

Exploration into God

> Affairs are now soul size
> The enterprise is exploration into
> God,
> Where are you making for?
> It takes so many thousand

years to wake
But will you wake for
pity's sake?
>From Christopher Fry, Sleep of Prisoners

Christopher Fry's ardent plea for the human heart to go to the lengths of God, calls for the awakening of dormant spiritual faculties in the soul that lie as seeds within soil. If these faculties were active in us we would be led to experience the world of spirit known to us before birth and in sleep, when soul and spirit return to their natural element. Rudolf Steiner describes this in the following passage:

> ...*how they shine forth with gentle phosphorescence, how they spread streaming warmth, how they speak out of their own essence, each spiritual form apparently different... The created world is nothing but the outer garment, the outer glory of creating hierarchies. Actual reality is only attained with knowledge of the spiritual beings at work in the various heavenly bodies... They are the true reality. Nothing else is real, neither space, nor time, nor matter.*

I learned from Dr. Steiner that for the spiritual world, earth is a kind of heaven and that if we are to be looked upon as the Gods of earth we need to assume a nobility of character. Older cultures were aware that it was their task to show the gods human things shining. Irish monks, for example, labored over illuminated manuscripts that their splendor might be commensurate with the Divine Word they contained. The angelic world only hearkens to *how* we approach a task and to our purity of *purpose* and the degree to which our human affairs are *ensouled* by love. Our simplest interactions with others, our sincerity, the quality of our gestures are full of spiritual significance.

Just as the caterpillar is born with the consciousness of the butterfly, so are we born with spiritual, fully human consciousness, inherent in us. What the caterpillar experienced as catastrophe within its cocoon, as it was pushed and pulled out of shape, appears in retrospect as the butterfly's appearance into form. We might apply the same analogy to ourselves only the process of metamorphosis in us is attended by witness, choice and therefore creative potential.

The Nature of the Soul

We have three distinctive aspects: body, soul and spirit. Manifestly obvious is our human form, the *body* whose senses provide a link with the surrounding world. In *soul* we experience the manner in which the environment reveals itself through pleasure, displeasure, desire and aversion. Through *spirit* we can regard the things of the world, from the point of view of their intrinsic value, leaving ourselves, our impressions and feelings out of the picture. Spirit is as different from the soul as soul is from the body. Both body and spirit come into play and connection through the soul. The delight I experience in looking up at the stars for instance belongs entirely to my own experience. The cosmic order and eternal laws of the stars, which I can think about, do not however belong to me, but to the stars themselves.

To him who is able to 'see' the soul, the radiance which proceeds from a human being because his eternal element is expanding, is just as much reality as the light which streams out from a flame is real to the physical eye.

From Rudolf Steiner

My body works its impressions into my soul through sensory experience. The more I move beyond self feeling, its subjective preoccupation, and align myself with eternal principles, the more the spiritual nature of my soul expands.

> ...A hyacinth in a glass it was,
> on my working table,
> Before my eyes opened beyond
> beauty lights pure living flow.
> 'It is I' I knew, 'I am that flower',
> that light is I,
> Both seer and sight...
>
> From Kathleen Raine, To the Sun

The light thus perceived by the awakened eye of poet Kathleen Raine is the reflection of her own luminous soul light generated in her lifelong devotion to nature.

Soul Development

There is a thread running from start to finish in every life story. Three phases can be discerned which reflect the evolution of earth itself - that of PARADISE, PARADISE LOST and PARADISE REGAINED. These stages are also in evidence in the way our souls develop from *sentient* to *intellectual* to *consciousness* soul. With an artist's divining perception, Yeats realized that a shift was taking place in twentieth century consciousness which he described as *the revolt of the soul against the intellect*.

He could sense that a force within the soul might yet supersede the dominance of the intellect. Sri Aurobindo, a westernized Eastern master known to Yeats wrote copiously at the same time about the birth of the *superconscious*, an inflow of higher knowing into the human psyche for which his own consciousness paved the way. Rudolf Steiner, their contemporary, termed this force *consciousness soul* and heralded its evolutionary development as spirit becoming aware of itself within human souls. Mythological and alchemical traditions have ever pointed towards a mystical marriage of soul and spirit. In religious circles it is referred to as the coming of the Holy Spirit. Writers of such prominence as Rufus Goodwin and Mark Patrick Hederman independently proclaim and chart the immanence in our world today of this third member of the Trinity. In Dr. Kühlewind's very succinct definition of the Trinity, the Son exists as the expression of the Father and the understanding of the Son constitutes the presence of Holy Spirit. The development of this faculty of the soul becomes most evident to me when intuition, which is to the intellect what breath is to the body, begins to lead one's life. Intuition is a spiritual faculty which guides without explanation and causes us to accept whatever is unfolding out of trust in a world being that is full of wisdom and mystery. I frequently utter the following affirmation as this faculty grows in me:

I am divinely sensitive to my intuitive leads,
and give instant obedience to Thy will.

Intuition and the synchronicity that attends it, gradually informs us of our participation in the greater order of things. In the Paradise period of earthly evolution ancient peoples experienced themselves to be at one with whatever they would apprehend, essentially in it and of it. I quote further lines of the Irish poet/seer quoted earlier in chapter three:

I am a boar for valor
I am a salmon in a pool
I am a lake on a plane
I am a word of science
I am the strength of art
I am a plant of beauty
    From Amergin's Song

This corresponds with the development of sentient soul mirrored in infancy. As babies we are as one with the sweet taste of the mother's milk, her warm and loving touch, the nursery sounds, rustling wind, the colors and nuances of light. The world first makes itself known through the senses, impinging by way of *sentient soul*.

Gradually as the child grows, a separation occurs and the Paradise Lost period begins, in the course of which independence can develop. Boundaries appear as *mine* and *yours* and *theirs*, 'I' emerging simultaneous with 'not I'. Information about the world as *other* is accumulated, reason employed. The desire to further one's own well-being awakens *intellectual soul*, the forces of which can be directed towards physical or spiritual concerns. As preoccupation with material life deepens, intellectual pursuits can begin to constitute a world in themselves. A world view can develop that excludes spiritual values, an exclusion of whatever is not visible or tangible or self serving. Knowing the price of everything and the value of nothing becomes our human lot. An over-identification with market values has led to the development of our economic, conformist and corporatist global society.

It was not as far advanced as it is today when Vaclav Havel addressed the following remarks to the World Economics Forum in the eighties:

> *The modern era has been dominated by the culminating belief, expressed in different forms, that the world - and Being as such - is a wholly knowable system governed by a finite number of universal laws that man can grasp and rationally direct for his own benefit. This era, beginning in the Renaissance and developing from the enlightenment to socialism from positivism to scientism from industrial revolution to the information revolution, was characterized by rapid advances in rational cognitive thinking.*
>
> *This in turn, gave rise to the proud belief in man as the pinnacle of everything that exists, and as possessing the one and only truth about the world. It was an era in which there was a cult of depersonalized objectivity, an era in which objective knowledge was*

amassed and technically exploited, an era of belief in automotive progress, brokered by the scientific method.
  From Vaclav Havel, World Economics Forum

The chasm between mind and heart which characterizes this modern world view, cannot ultimately be bridged by the acquisition of more knowledge and things, wants exceeding needs, satiation in the place of satisfaction. We are called to witness rather than judge, remaining open to the time spirit from the future. Such an opening has always been present in the psyche of artists traditionally not bound by the spell of convention and they are models for us now. The development of *consciousness soul* requires that we cultivate an attitude of open attention towards that-which-is-not-yet. If we are resistant to the new and unpredictable, it often takes the shock of a crisis, illness or other unexpected event to challenge popular assumptions whether religious, political or cultural. A person, a book, a film, a work of art or an invitation may introduce a change of heart. The jargon of politics, evangelism and the popular media is found wanting when one questions the very purpose of life, when one's identity is shattered for one reason or another. For a time familiar words cannot carry us, but poetic consciousness I believe, ultimately can.

Dying and Becoming

I met Samuel Beckett in Paris in 1973. My late husband was there and the actress Siobhán McKenna. He struck me as ascetic, kind and humble.

You must go on, I can't go on, I'll go on, you must say the words, as long as there are any, until they find me, until they say me, strange pain, strange sin, you must go on, perhaps its done already, perhaps they have carried me to the threshold of my story, before the door that opens on my story, that would surprise me, if it opens it will be I, it will be the silence where I am, I don't know, I'll never know,

Treasa O'Driscoll

> *in the silence you don't know, you must go on, I can't go on, I'll go on.*
>
> From Samuel Beckett, The Unnameable

Despondency and lack may be the hallmark of the characters in Beckett's novels, but the economy and style of his writing, the comic twists given to the worst aspects of human circumstances, lifts his work above pathos. His art redeems his exposition of the bleakness of the human condition and is indeed an antidote to the torments and fantasies that bedevil human minds, a mirror of which Beckett holds up to the world. Some mutual friends had arranged the meeting, friends who always spoke of him in reverential tones. I could understand his publisher's tribute to Beckett on his sixtieth birthday.

> *"In all my life I have never met a man in whom co-exist together in such high degree nobility and modesty, lucidity and goodness."*

The great teachers of mankind have often incarnated to work as artists and influence people's consciousness in subtle and non-dogmatic ways and Beckett belongs in this category.

The contemporary teacher I most admire, Mother Meera, holds silent darshan for the thousands who flock to her home in Germany. I have direct experience of the inner state of certainty and peace that can be experienced through her presence. I am grateful for the following words that appeared in a book of her teachings:

> *Try to be wise enough to know that you do not know. Then the Divine can lead you forward into true knowledge, calmly, stage by stage. Give me your mind without fear and I will expand it. When the heart suffers, it is easy to transform its suffering into joy, but when the mind creates and lives a fantasy, it is extremely hard to change it. So be careful. Do not let your mind become your worst enemy.*
>
> From Mother Meera, Answers

Today we witness the devastation brought about by the collapse of outmoded regimes, internecine tribal warfare, corrupt government and wayward living. Mother Meera offers words of comfort in the face of inevitable change:

> *To achieve realization a dying to the old self is necessary. But why be sad about it? What has the old self given you that you should love it so? The divine self will give you all things and also give you bliss. Do not think in terms of "giving up" anything. Think of growing stronger and more loving and more complete. Then what you wanted yesterday you will not want today and what you wanted today, tomorrow you will see is not useful. Discipline must be there and control - not in the name of "death" but in the name of love and true life.*

The Divine presence makes itself known whenever we open our hearts to its healing influence.

> ...*You* be the master, make yourself
> fierce
> Break in and then your great
> Transforming will happen to me
> And my great grief cry will
> happen to you.
>   Rainer Maria Rilke (translation by Robert Bly)

To withstand an environment saturated with fear and terror we must cultivate an unshakable firmness and inner certainty. The study of the Gospels, absorbing the very deepest of what can be experienced of their content, gives one this inner firmness and fills the void with a feeling of courage. In my own experience the memorization of poetry and passages from sacred texts also provide great inner ballast against depression and despair.

Awakening to Consciousness Soul

The *Paradise Lost* period of growth precedes the awakening of consciousness soul, by which the intellectual and sentient soul become transfigured by the spiritual permeation of a more intuitive order of knowing. What has often been referred to as the second birth arises of its own necessity. An awakened intuitiveness, enlivened intellect and enriched sensory experience characterizes the life that opens up when Paradise comes within reach again. The world may still be the same but our perception of it will have radically altered as when the illumination of daylight dispels the mantle of darkness. This characterizes the awakening of consciousness soul in us. It is our original memory of Paradise that propels us towards the conscious regaining of it. Parzival's encounter with knights in shining armor in the forest as a boy, caused him to abandon his mother and the life of safety she represented in pursuit of the flashing vision of Paradise reflected in sunlight on shields. These flashes come when we give our attention to the people and places to which we are innately related by predisposition. It is by means of the eternal law of karma that the spirit of the world draws forth the deepest spirit in mankind.

A man is a method, a progressive arrangement; a selecting principle, gathering his like to him wherever he goes. He takes only his own out of the multiplicity that sweeps and circles around him…

From Emerson

Desire leads us to discover what aspect of Paradise seeks to reveal itself in us, through us to the world. The impulse towards renewal in the social sphere comes at the prompting of consciousness soul. Because we are bearers of love we have a desire to understand people and events. At the same time there is a tendency in each one to regard her or himself as the standard of what is right. Whenever we disagree with someone it is often based in a subconscious prejudice that dictates *this person should be more like me*! Every urge we have to reform others stems from this approach. Oscar Wilde remarked incisively: *Selfishness is not living as one wishes to live, it is asking others to live as one wishes to live.*

In cultivating a speech of the grail, a speech that arises out of an inner listening, we become aware of the negativity that can permeate conversation and the character assassination which fuels gossip. Speech is closer to us than any other form of expression and guarding the tongue is crucial in the development of consciousness soul.

> *One should arrive at leading one's conscience to a state of development so that it becomes the voice of a better and higher self of which the ordinary self is a servant.*
> From Vincent Van Gogh

Whenever we take the smallest steps in the direction suggested by Van Gogh, there is a simultaneous gesture of helpfulness extended towards us from invisible benefactors.

> *Yes, when I work, when I am submissive and modest, I feel myself so helped by someone who makes me do things that surpass me.*
> From Henri Matisse

Bearing in mind the spiritual activity of the beings of creation described by Rudolf Steiner, we can understand Beethoven's response to a question regarding the origins of his musical ideas:

> *They come to me in the silence of the night or in the early morning, stirred into being by moods which the poet could translate into words but which I could put into sounds and these grow through my head. Ringing and singing and storming until at last I have them before me as notes.*

In another context the great composer admitted that there was no loftier mission than to approach the Godhead as closely as he did and by means of that contact, to spread the ways of the Godhead through the human race.

Artists have always instructed us in the source, the ideas, the meaning of life. They teach us about the play of our mental faculties and about the need to play as children play, calling forth the artist in each one of us and awakening the hero within each soul. We are guided in the return to Paradise by our love of beauty, innate in everybody but often suppressed, smothered, thwarted.

Love is no more than action at the level of the physical body, idea at the level of the mind and beauty at the level of feelings. The lover, Plotinus says, is stabbed with delight at the beauty of the body. He is also the one who feels the deepest wounds having a heightened sense of beauty's essential simplicity and purity, which exactly matches its end as the mean of all extremes. Beauty is that balance we fleetingly apprehend and ever strive towards. I believe that this striving and that apprehension is the essence of love and the wonderful fact is that as human beings we experience it through one another, art being its mirror, a means through which we keep a steady focus on the essential. The awakening to *consciousness soul* is at the same time an awakening in love, as the force which binds and orders the universe. Life now begins to open up to include and transmute the death forces that dog us as shadows of habit and prejudice, when purer and truer forces are breaking into consciousness. In this way we embark on an art of living in which the most common and everyday tasks can be raised up. The hero within is the artist within who can understand.

> *Art is a way of life faithful to the natural instincts and therefore faithful to childhood; not any self control or self limitation for the sake of specific ends, but rather a careful letting go of oneself; not*

caution but rather a wise blindness not working to acquire silent, slowly increasing possessions, but rather a continuous squandering of all perishable values. This way of being has something naive and instinctive about it and resembles that period of the unconscious best characterized by a joyous confidence, namely the period of childhood.

From Rilke

When we are admonished to become as little children in order to enter the Kingdom of Heaven we are, in the deepest sense, being invited to become artists, revealers of the laws of beauty which make themselves known through a depth of feeling, always the mark of genius. "Do you go very far from the sea and the earth?" Children once enquired of Lorca in a Spanish market square. "I will go very far, he replied, further than those hi*lls,* further than the sea, close to the stars, to ask Christ the Lord to give me back my ancient soul of a child, mellowed with legends."

> *To be great be entire:*
> *Of what is yours nothing exaggerate or exclude*
> *Be whole in each thing. Put all you are into the least you do*
> *Like that on each place the whole moon*
> *Shines for she lives aloft.*
> *Fernando Pessoa*

Ten

ENTERING THE OVERLAP ZONE

Today we are called upon to adopt a meditative approach to every task we perform. Not only is this an antidote for stress, it awakens in each heart a love for simple things, a gratitude for the natural bounty of the earth, for the gift of consciousness.

Two monks called Kevin and Ciaran, have the following exchange as they peel potatoes:

> *Kevin: Being spiritual is thinking about spiritual things while peeling potatoes!*

> *Ciaran: Being spiritual is thinking about peeling potatoes while peeling potatoes!*

The meditative approach implies the giving of equal value to people and to tasks, a coming into rhythm with ourselves and the world around us. We begin to have the experience of pilgrims, a sense of operating in two dimensions simultaneously. Passing human time which we can measure by the clock is contained and unfolds always within the dimension of the eternal. Eternal time floods through human time, introducing transcendent elements such as synchronicity, and coincidence. We enter eternal time whenever we meet a significant other. Monastic life with its rhythm of prayer, work and worship can also give entry to this *overlap zone* in which earthly consciousness can be fused with the heavenly. For many people the practice of meditative mindfulness develops out of an eastern discipline which brings about an expansion in consciousness to free the individual from the obsessive and narrow focus of habitual desire. Attention has to move from grasping to open. This is sometimes referred to as the tantric path. Tantra implies becoming conscious in thought, word and deed. It is a highly evolved form of love as play.

Master storyteller Osho, related how Tantra arose as a path. Central to the tale was Saraha, the son of a learned Brahmin. A Buddhist monk, he had a vision of the woman who would become his teacher.

"You will need the cooperation of a wise woman to enter into the complex world of Tantra. Tantra flourishes in the thick of life... Saraha went to the marketplace... He found the woman he had seen in the vision... She was an arrowsmith woman of low caste and Saraha belonged to a line of learned Brahmins."

"The learned has to go to the vital. The plastic has to go to the real."

The woman was radiant with life, wholly absorbed in the making of an arrow.

"He immediately felt something extraordinary in her presence, something that he had never come across. Even Sri Kirti, his master, paled before the presence of this woman. Something so fresh and something from the very source..."

He watched her carefully as she assumed the posture of aiming at an invisible target. Her ease and concentration had a magnetic effect upon him. But she laughed derisively at him when he asked her a question. Noting his yellow robes she said:

"You think you are a Buddhist? Buddha's meaning can only be known through actions, not through words and not through books. Is it not enough for you? Are you not fed up with all this? Do not waste any more time in that futile search. Come and follow me!"

The woman was beautiful but her beauty had come through total absorption. Her grace and her beauty were the result of balance and freedom from extremes. Watching her, Saraha surrendered. He understood for the first time what meditation is. He had noticed her closing one eye and opening another - a Buddhist symbol.

"She had closed one eye as symbolic of the eye of reason and logic. And she had opened the other eye symbolic of love, intuition, awareness. And her aim was towards the unknown, the invisible, the unknowable."

Saraha became a *tantrika* under the woman's guidance. He entered into the soul love affair of disciple and master, into a love so great that it rarely happens on earth. Now, concluded Osho:

"He no longer meditates. He sings of course, and dances too. Now singing was his meditation. Now celebration was his whole lifestyle... Play entered into his being and through play, true religion was born."

Little did I know, when I first heard this story that I would, many years later, meet somebody who would have a similar effect on me. I had to fall in love with a teacher who would demonstrate in the most simple and practical ways what it means to be in heaven and on earth at the same time ...

Meeting a New Man

I had lived in Vancouver for almost two years before I met Claude. On a wet Sunday afternoon in April I ventured across town on the hunch that I was to meet someone... I drove resolutely in the direction of Banyen Books, the city's most popular bookstore and a favorite haunt of mine. As I walked in I saw that the window bench from which I often bookwormed my way through endless volumes, was empty. Ignoring the tempting display of books for once, I sat expectantly in my usual spot. Within minutes I was catching a flash of the sunniest smile I had ever seen. It illumined the clear-eyed, bearded face of an elegantly clad and handsome man in his late forties. Of slight but noble stature, he appeared to acknowledge me energetically as he rounded a nearby bookcase. *The heart went crossways in me*, as we used to say when I was growing up in Galway. I had to exercise great restraint in not running after him to breathlessly ask:

Who are you? Do I know you?
Have we met before?

How do you come to be so fine, so graceful, so noble, so light on your feet, to have such an air of savoir faire, savoir vivre, of wisdom, of happiness...?

Instead I remained rooted to the spot. Then I noticed he had spirited himself to the position of sitting next to me on the bench, and seemed to be quietly observing me without looking... Taking me in as it were... Silence reigned in which I could hear my heart beating... I self-consciously rose and began to leaf through a book, absentmindedly plucked from a bookshelf. I soon became aware of a presence behind me... in a quiet voice and with a slight accent he spoke.

"I must speak to you. Will you join me for a coffee?"

A world of possibility hovered around our corner of the cafe as we became acquainted. It was much later, that I realized how appropriate his surname was. Bellin— from *belle*, but also connoting bell; *clear and sound as a bell*, having *the ring of truth*. He told me he had come from Nice to visit his brother. He had lived in Vancouver for many years, but he had returned to settle in the south of France where he was born. I noted that his English was as fluent as my own, his diction and vocabulary distinctive and expressive. We agreed to meet later that evening and continued to rendezvous until the day of his departure dawned, a week later.

There were no 'facts' about him to cling to, nothing that was familiar. His background was a mystery, although we did oddly, have one acquaintance in common. A singer friend-of-a-friend in Toronto, had once mentioned in passing that she had lived with a Frenchman named Claude in Vancouver... I was bound to him from the start by intangibles— his sense of life, an ease of manner, a quality of centered calmness, a lack of pretense, clarity of mind, my happiness in his presence... Whatever the attraction was,

I missed him when he left, after the first of several tearful airport scenes. I will always cherish him as we meet and part in one country or another, indefinitely. For some time I thought I could not live without him, but gradually discovered I could be happy whether he was there or not. As we crossed the threshold of the usual man/woman resistance to surrender, it became clear to each of us that a conventional mating was not in the Divine plan for us. The dialogue we have with one another is timeless, the unpredictable quality of life itself dictates that there be no last word between us. The wonder of love is that it keeps us in the flow of that which is alive, deeply interested in all the loved one's possible unfolding.

> Love's ordained priest
> you bade me drink
> Deeply of the cup of life,
> nectar of the here and now
> Source of the seamless
> ordering of time and space
> The fitness of things
> coming moment to moment
> To light, in thought and word
> and deed
> love expands the way before us
> Her enterprise ours as we meet and part and meet again
> Living the mystery. Namaste!

I abandoned other interests to spend an intense period of time living with Claude in Vancouver. Working for a few hours a day in exchange for rent, we were installed as caretakers in a large Vancouver mansion while Claude recovered from a minor operation. A part of every day was spent walking in one of the lush forests in or around Vancouver. Claude moved in and out of what I term the overlap zone. The more I grew to love and trust him the more my experience of what he referred to as *Real Time*, increased. My induction was a slow process and largely due to his patient guidance and constant reminders to "be here now!," whenever I drifted into past or future preoccupation. I learned by his example how to enter into the rhythm of "nature's time" as he called it, as he drew my attention to all the small wonders with which we were surrounded. As we ducked under branches and rooted out trails he urged me to move with open attention, seeing and hearing with greater sensitivity, looking and listening in a more relaxed way. A favorite poem became truly meaningful for me then and a metaphor for life.

> ...Stand still, The trees ahead and the bushes beside you
> Are not lost. Wherever you are is called Here,
> And you must treat it as a powerful stranger,
> Must ask permission to know it and be known...
> From David Wagoner, Lost.

He explained that he first entered into the continuity of real time when he was twenty nine, becoming aware of the closeness of the spiritual world to our sphere of activity, a parallel world in contact with ours all the time. He approached the subject of Real Time, so dear to his heart, in several different ways.

"I know deep down that nothing else but real time exists. You have to accept this universal unfolding and realize once and for all that the past is a dead thing—only as good as a slide that you would project on the wall of your mind. And the future, as beautiful as you can envisage it, is also a diversion from the living experience which is always in the making. We know that, in these difficult times reality is a hard thing for people to accept. But once the reality is tamed it is accepted and seen to be beautiful. You have no more need for fairy tales. I find that life is truly magical when lived in the moment. What I am asking you is not to be so caught up in your own agendas, associations, just concentrate always on what you are doing. I am not asking you to discard anything. I am inviting you to pay much more attention to the seconds that are passing you by. To be here now is to be conscious."

"How do I make a shift into Real Time?" I asked.

"You have to shift from *your* importance to the importance of life itself."

"Isn't our presence part of the life force?"

"No" he countered "It is the life force. That is what is demanded of us."

"We think if we are sitting in a chair, we are present" I said.

Claude smiled, "Sometimes the lights are on but there is nobody home."

"Children are always present" I said.

"When we are present we are childlike" he responded.

Claude always had something to do, the concept of boredom was entirely alien to him as he busied himself with household tasks. His hands, small and strong had their history of a life in which everything is present and alive to the touch. Since he first undertook the milking of goats as a very young boy he had been nicknamed 'golden hands'. These hands retained their youthful readiness and inner vitality of gesture and touch. Inspiration always flowed into his hands. Every task called forth in him an inner wholehearted response and he would cheerfully spring into action. He made no distinction of interest between intellectual or artistic pursuits and mundane household chores. All were important in the rhythmic flow of the day.

He was total in action and always brought what he started to satisfactory completion without too much fuss or strain. Because he set such value on himself he gave value to all he did. An unhurried calmness showed him the way in every act of repairing, cleaning, cooking, carving, drumming, painting or gardening. I thought as I watched him: *Here is the truth of right doing*, fervently wishing that I could do likewise. Because I have so internalized the memory of his speech and gestures, snippets of conversation come back to me. I hear him say:

"The more you are centered in what you do and how you are doing it, the more *before* and *after* become uninteresting. Because love is at work."

"Love?" I query.

"Yes. If you are so involved of your own volition, it is because your heart is in it and love is in everything you do."

Home Ground

People are an invisible element of a place made visible, Wallace Stevens said in a poem. In this way Provence became visible for me through Claude before I ever set foot in that earthly paradise. There, was realized the perfect setting for the jewel of such splendor that my friend represented for me. His home town Nice, playground to the rich and famous presents a commercial face to the tourist. Although his love of finery and well-made things has been fostered there, he has not followed the lure of riches. A drive into the hills, beyond Nice, presents another reality. Taking a detour one day in the course of my first visit, he drove along a winding path and stopped at a little river, the stream from which he had drawn water daily as a boy. Remote by an hour's walk from the nearest neighbor, he showed me the ruin of a modest house, in the attic of which he had bedded on a straw mattress for the first nine years of his life. He had been reared a solitary child in the care of an elderly couple. Like a small animal himself, he passed the days in the company of cats and dogs and goats and chickens, communing with birds from the branches of gnarled olive trees. He laughed when I remarked: "You were as wild here as you later became as a city dweller, abandoning yourself to fast cars, dance halls and the arms of women, as you had earlier to wind and earth and branch!"

Never setting eye on pen or paper when other children were swotting over books, Claude was instructed by volatile winds, rocks and flowers and subtle seasonal change. No wonder he said when I asked him once how he would define freedom: "To be on holiday when others are at work!" Here he absorbed into his own being the patience and calmness and innate kindness of nature herself, it was a book which would always remain open to him. Being yourself, being natural is all that is needed, he would remind me. From early childhood he knew what it was to be independent and yet function as part of the whole. "People lose faith when they have lost their link with the world around them. I once had the feeling as a small child that I might get lost on my wanderings in this region. But I was told, 'only follow the river and you will find your way home'. In this way I learned to find my bearings wherever I went." He had been busy from morning until night in this secluded domain, collecting pine cones to start a morning fire, watering the vegetables that were their staple diet, carrying water in which to boil the homemade pasta.

"They told me – If you want your dinner you must chop wood!"

Everything was used and everything had meaning, his intolerance of waste and remarkable resourcefulness was seeded here. He had a special relationship with trees and told me," If I had a choice I would become a cork tree. It does not yield any fruit but gives of itself continuously." From brick red to dusty ochre he learned the merits of every soil, the qualities of wood that would inform his skills as carver and carpenter.

"When my two older brothers came to visit from the city, we would make boats from the bark of a tree, bows with new branches of the chestnut tree, arrows from the stems of ferns. My only toys were the ones I invented myself."

"I saw how different plants grew according to season. I welcomed the appearance of new mushrooms, wild asparagus and lettuce. I was always asking 'What new thing can we find to eat?' Whenever a need arose I could find a solution."

"You learned the value of animals too," I said.

"Up to this day I have a hard time understanding why people have animals for decoration - all the animals had a purpose for us, the cats for mice and insects, the dogs for sheep. I vividly remember seeing little chicks playing on the cat's back! I walked for five miles to the village exchanging goats milk, cheese and rabbits for oil and flour."

Although he swears that he has never eaten as well since, his excitement in the marketplace had all the fervor of childhood. Surveying the abundant provision of colorful produce, ripened in the golden glow of direct Mediterranean sunlight I could understand his frustration with the insipid look and smell of vegetables in other places. The Provencal dishes he had so painstakingly prepared for us in Vancouver paled beside the home grown gastronomic marvels he set before me now. The glistening fish lightly cooked, pan roasted duck or corn-fed chickens, baby courgettes, mouth-watering blette, flour-drenched fresh pasta, vine-ripe tomatoes, an endless variety of cheeses, highly-scented orange-fleshed melons, and other juicy fruits, were just some of the fare that found a place at our table. The aroma of rosemary, thyme, sage and lavender which hung over the surrounding hills made a subtle transition from nostril to palate through the magic of Claude's hands. He showed me how to pick out the best of those cornerstones of Provencal cuisine, olive oil, garlic and thyme and how to add their flavors so that no one taste stands out above another. "Faites simple" was his motto and each culinary achievement was punctuated with "Voila!"

We often drove by narrow twisting roads along hills topped by mediaeval villages. I remember flashes of the cornucopia of markets, patisseries, fromageries, boulangeries, baroque churches, almond, plum and fig orchards... We saw elderly men playing petanque in dusty village squares, others sampling a little pastis—the quintessential Provencal aperitif—in the outdoor cafes that dotted cobbled streets. Ochre and red-washed walls reflected the surrounding soil, their red tiled roofs offset by the expanse of azure sky. Ancient limestone buildings rose organically from the rocky pinnacles of distant heights. There was always an olive grove where we could stop to picnic. Everything I experienced served to explain the great leap my heart took when I first set eyes on Claude. Here indeed was life abundantly overflowing its limitations; my definition for peace. No wonder the olive branch was adopted as its symbol. It had originally been borne on the wings of a dove to Noah as proof of the existence of dry land, synonymous for him at the time I suppose with his particular vision of Paradise.

For Wisdom's Sake

Claude does not espouse any particular religion, he was baptized a Catholic, but was never taken to church as a child. He once was given a vision of the Light, and holds a strong Christian identity. His keen ability to interpret the Tarot symbols gives him Hermetic lineage. He would make no claim beyond the development of his own conscious awareness. The only prayerful request he remembers making in his youth was for the gift of wisdom, the gift of recognizing Heaven's hiddenness within this world. Like Fionn Mac Cumhail, he would go anywhere and forsake anything for wisdom. Words attributed to Philo of Alexandria seem relevant to my description of Claude: *If someone has experienced the wisdom that can only be heard from oneself, learned from oneself, and created from oneself, he does not merely participate in laughter, he becomes laughter.* Whether in Canada, in Ireland or in France, my favorite time of day with Claude began immediately after breakfast when he would hold forth with astonishing clarity on some topic that might arise out of a simple comment.

"Thoughts are something active, living, the working forces of the world. We simply draw them out of the world."

There was no gap for him between thought and word. His thoughts issued forth with complete originality, born of the moment and clothed in the most appropriate and incisive language. I asked him how we could tell if a statement was really true. "If it is truth', he expostulated, "it is alive! When you apprehend this truth, this energy, it is something cosmic, divine—you've been allowed to enter a realm of Reality, piercing through the veil of illusion. *The truth will set you free* means it will give you life."

"Becoming conversant with the world consciousness involves continuous *conversation*. You come up with new questions all the time. You can start anywhere!"

The most recent conversation I have had with him which was not conducted at great expense over the phone, was when last I spent a few weeks with him in Nice. Like all the conversations we had shared in the twelve years of our association, it had neither beginning nor end and was plucked from the ether as usual, highlighting some aspect of life-wisdom. It gave me entry once more into the overlap zone. We were talking about the way in which thoughts were subconsciously transmitted from one person to another and how becoming conscious of what we say could help us bring order into our thinking. He had this to offer: "Words cannot do total justice to the fine thoughts we have. They are often a pale reflection of our ongoing reality. You must first have a grasp of what you are saying. Be completely honest. Describe the situation in real terms clearly and accurately without adding or subtracting. Concern yourself with your description of reality without judging or belittling, with a maximum of restraint. In practicing this, little by little, you will notice that your thoughts have been disorderly. The more you give order to the words you speak the more you are training your thoughts. Your subconscious is recording everything accurately, becoming now a reservoir of orderly thinking patterns. Your surroundings in turn, will begin to reflect this reality."

"So," he continued animatedly, "one of my approaches on the spiritual path is to be vigilant about my speaking."

I encouraged him to elaborate.

"It entails really searching for the word that is clearest and most true and usually the simplest, saying 'no' when you mean 'no' and 'yes' when you mean 'yes'."

"Saying exactly what you mean and meaning what you say," I interjected.

"Yes," he continued, "in this way I become a more responsible person, able to stand behind my words. Instead of my thoughts giving form to my speech in a haphazard way, my speech now begins to influence my subconscious and one of the functions of the subconscious is to release information. If I am attentive and vigilant in what I say, my thoughts will have no choice but to sift themselves and what will remain of that purifying process is the essence of what I feel and now succinctly convey."

"But does that make you more readily understood by others?" I asked.

His answer surprised me.

"It is not important to be understood. It is not important whether or not people agree with me. It is important that I am convinced about my point of view. Because if I am not convinced I will always be on shaky ground. I will drift from one approach to another. Before I start to speak I must have a point of view—a position."

"How would you advocate arriving at a position?" I queried.

"I arrive at it through many channels, education, knowledge, the love of parents, equilibrium, integrity of character—by whatever means the truth can be in motion within."

"Is experience important?" I asked.

"Fundamental truth bypasses experience. It is connected with faith and it is based on something more solid than anything I have learned from books or seen on television, or read in the newspaper. All of that only forms opinions. A point of view, on the other hand is based on reasoning and a concept of truth which I would term intuition, a concept of light which I would call imagination and a concept of love functioning as compassion.

"When these three facets are in place for some time, lets say for a cycle of nine years, I will then have learned a great deal about limits, about access (in terms of being able to receive images), about excess (in terms of being over emotional), and limits (in terms of what may or may not be spoken). Now my point of view becomes truly referential. Now I am convinced that I can add something of substance to a situation and I have left opinion behind on the sidewalk!"

Claude once made the point that humanity made its start when it learned to generate fire. The current force analogous to fire, with which humanity is now charged to generate, is that of Love.

"Love changes everything. It inevitably changes the nature of what is happening, for the good. Our task is to be able to see love everywhere. We must become receptive enough to be able to facilitate the coming of such a force."

He constitutes such a force in my life.

> *We are only just now beginning to consider the relation of one individual to a second individual objectively and without prejudice, and our attempts to live such relationships have no model before them. And yet in the changes brought about by time there are already many things that can help our timid novitiate...*
> *Rainer Maria Rilke.*

Eleven

EMBRACING THE DREAM

We evolve towards complimentarity only gradually, arriving there by means of one partner or several. Ideals which reflect cherished aspirations will not appear manifest in the ones we attract, however high our hopes, until they first come to light in ourselves.

Relationships are experiments in love to which we need not attach yardsticks of success or failure, love has a way of placing such inducements in our path so that individuality may ripen in us for the sake of one another, that the world may benefit.

"I think the hero in our generation is not the individual but the pair, two people who together add up to more than they are apart."
From Theodore Zeldin, BBC radio commentary.

Zeldin is a writer who promotes a contemporary model of male/female relationship, based on the art of conversation.

I learned by way of trial and error that although love is unconditional, relationship flourishes when clear conditions are mutually agreed upon and individual boundaries recognized and respected.

"My freedom stops," Claude once remarked, "where yours begins, and vice versa."

To be loved in spite of our flaws implies that these imperfections must become transparent to lovers. Concealing them, ironically sets up barriers which obstruct the course of love. One can wait forever for the perfect mate as did an elderly Irish bachelor who confessed to me his regret at never having married. I asked him "Why not?"

He said "Well it was not for want of trying..... I have known women throughout the length and breadth of the country."

"You mean you have been looking around?"

"Yes—I met a woman once in Limerick. She was beautiful, she was wealthy, but she was not religious, so I dropped her after a while."

"Where did you go then?" I asked.

"I ventured on to Cork and there I met the finest, most religious girl. But although she was beautiful she had no money."

"I suppose you moved on from her too?"

"After that I met someone I liked in Galway but she was not much to look at."

"But still you persisted?"

"Yes indeed. I worked for a while in Dublin where there is a surplus of women. Sure enough I walked out with one who had a good income, who was lovely to look at and spiritual into the bargain."

"It's a wonder you didn't marry her." I remarked

"The unfortunate thing with her was, and it is the reason I gave up the chase—she was looking for the perfect man!"

I understand why popular songs have always sounded the theme—*The greatest thing you'll ever learn is just to love and be loved in return.*

One of the first love stories to catch my schoolgirl fancy was the mythological account of the meeting and mating of the hero Cuchulainn with Emer, the only noblewoman in Ireland worthy of his attentions. She in turn recognized him instantly as the man of her dreams. An old book gave account of their first meeting:

"May the Lord make straight the paths before you," were her words of greeting when she lifted her lovely face to gaze into his eyes for the first time.

"And you—may you be safe from every harm," he replied.

The spontaneous concern of each was for the other's well-being. This is a sign of true love. The love that is protected from every base instinct is the love for one another that is for the other's own sake.

"From whence have you come?" she inquired and she had lineage as well as route in mind. As he alighted from his chariot to move closer to her she became mesmerized by his presence. It was well known that he had, what in Irish we term, *an ball seirce,* and which in Sufi terms must be *the jewel of reality.*

> Nobody can wear the jewel of reality
> Except the one in whose fire it is born
> My friend wears it on his forehead
> Our foreheads touched tonight and mine burns.
> From Rumi

I believe that this potential third eye can be awakened by lovers in one another. Love itself must become the guide, not expectation or convention. Emer did not exact a vow of faithfulness from Cuchulainn before its time. Her response to his proposal exacted tests of strength, resolve and daring. His manly instincts would have to be tempered in the crucible of her loving heart before loyalty and faithfulness would arise of their own accord to refine his wilfulness as infinitely renewable virtues.

When Emer outlined her accomplishments for Cuchulainn during their first meeting she included the following gifts of womanhood—loveliness, sweet and pleasant speech, the gifts of handiwork, purity and wisdom. Cuchulainn identified a further quality.

"Yet I see one excellence you have not noted in your speech. Never before this day among all women with whom I have at times conversed, have I found one but thee to speak the mystic language of the bards which we are talking now for secrecy one with the other."

We can allow a space to open up in our conversations which gives expression to the subtitles that often underlie our encounters so that judgement, the obscure, the hidden and the unsayable can be aired without fear. This requires courage and practice and authenticity. Monsieur Zeldin argues that, "whenever words dance with each other, opinions caress, imaginations undress, topics open..."

Treasa O'Driscoll

Midnight Courting

When I was young it was not unusual for couples to be engaged for fourteen years before conditions favorable to marriage could be adapted to their circumstances. We used to joke about farmers in our area, leaning over their shovels, squinting after the young girls on summer evenings, thinking to themselves, "Isn't it great to be sixty and to be old enough to go courting!" The delay was due to the fact that a farm could only withstand one mistress and it was not until after the death of his mother that a son could contemplate bringing another woman into the house. The indispensable tradition of matchmaking, to which such hopefuls could then resort when the desire for a mate became urgent, is still a feature of life in County Clare. Lisdoonvarna, a town famous for its healing waters, is a popular meeting and matchmaking centre which now attracts the unattached but available of both genders from every corner of the earth.

Clare has featured in my life since early childhood when I used to spend summer holidays here with relatives. But I did not appreciate the richness of its topography until my late husband and I began to frequent annual *Merriman* summer schools in the late sixties and early seventies when a gathering of scholars, artists and politicians could be wholeheartedly at home in the rural ambience of County Clare. Set-dancing sometimes began at ten in the morning and it was a popular alternative to lectures as were the absorbing conversations in session in every corner of the pubs. It was at these affairs that I learned to perfect the art of hanging out.

Background or foreground reels and jigs gave way when a singer was present. I shall always remember the energetic and soaring rendition of great Munster songs by one of Ireland's most popular historians, John A. Murphy.

The highlights of our days were the field trips we took with archaeologists, whose knowledge of all the treasures of the landscape was exhaustive, delivered on site to a thoroughly captivated audience. Thus did remnants of monument and stone begin to more fully inhabit the locality again through the imaginative associations we gave them. These trips gave living testimony to Yeats' contention that in this land *every strange stone and little coppice has its legend in written or unwritten tradition.*

The book *The Antiquities in Clare* includes a translation of the Gaelic poem *The Midnight Court*, which was written by Brian Merriman in 1790. At that time, Merriman was a hedge-school master in the village of Feakle, some twenty minutes drive from my present writing place. It is this poem of some one thousand lines that drew us to County Clare every year. It has held sway with social historians, literary critics, censorship boards and the general reader for over two hundred years. Deploring repression, women's inequality, clerical celibacy, the poem advocates unrestrained heterosexual activity between consenting adults. For one critic this gives evidence that a primitive form of erotic life had held its vigor in rural Ireland. A young woman gives petulant voice to a litany of superstitious and magical rites that she employed to gain the attention of a man.

   ...Every night as I went to bed
   I'd a stocking of apples under my head,
   I fasted three canonical hours
   To try and come round the heavenly powers,
   I washed my shift where the stream ran deep,
   To hear my lover's voice in sleep;

Treasa O'Driscoll

> Often I swept the woodstack bare,
> Burned bits of my frock, my nails, my hair,
> Up the chimney stuck the flail,
> Slept with a spade without avail...
>> From The Midnight Court
>> translated by Frank O'Connor

A Tremor of the Future

Seamus Heaney points out in a learned essay on *The Midnight Court* that the poem can be read as *a tremor of the future* and recognizes it as an original and unexpected achievement from the perspective of world literature of the eighteenth century. A parody of the *Aisling* [vision] poetic convention of that period, the poet exults in the scenic beauty of his native place in the lyrical opening verses. But he is not visited by the customary ethereal beauty, that personification of the Irish folk spirit, but is rudely accosted by a grotesque female figure who demands that he appear at a special court to be convened at midnight near the village of Feakle. Presiding over this tribunal is Aoibheall (pronounced Eevel) a formidable fairy queen who resides in Craglea. (Craglea is not far from Tinarana. It is a tall grey rock that juts out of the mountain where I pass on my daily walks). Merriman is being held accountable for the failings of his sex, chapter and verse of which are passionately proclaimed by an array of female witnesses. He is denounced and condemned to torture by a pack of these feminists-before-their-time, a nightmare he escapes by waking up.

I have had to look beyond the Irish psyche and the attitudes of my own conditioning to discover what Heaney's *tremor* might indicate. I was led at first to Vladimir Solovyov, a mystical Russian prophet and Christian metaphysician who wrote at the turn of the twentieth century. During his short lifetime he advanced a powerful social message concerning the love between man and woman. The transformation of the world, he believed, depended upon this relationship and the evolutionary channel it represented. His approach to the subject in his book *The Meaning of Love,* is earnestly scientific, opening with a biological survey which refutes the age old presumption that the fundamental purpose of sexual attraction is the propagation of the species. He proves that the higher we ascend in the hierarchy of organisms, the more this purpose wanes but the more urgent the power of sexual attraction becomes. He calls for the exaltation of the sexual instinct, behind which spiritual powers operate.

The meaning and worth of love as a feeling is that it really forces us, with all our being, to acknowledge for another the same absolute significance which, because of the power of egoism, we are conscious of only in our own selves. Love is important not only as one of our feelings, but as the transfer of all our interest in life from ourselves to another, as the shifting of the very centre of our lives.

The poet Coleridge was also aware of the necessary interpenetration of love and egoism and Steiner argued that one should not suppress the other, but be eternally engaged in a movement towards the union of opposites. All unity implies working through the resistance through which the ego perpetuates itself. For a couple to mutually surrender to the current of sexual love on a continuing basis implies an overcoming of the limiting definitions we hold of ourselves. Solovyov believed that no external influences however beneficial could touch the roots of egoism in us which only the momentum of the sexual act could undermine. In this form of love, penetrating as it does the whole of our being, we can recognize the truth of another, not merely in abstraction or in feeling, but in actual deed as the justification of our inborn capacity to love.

Thus we are called to the conscious task of love as a duty of our humanity and the goal of our evolution. The physical act of love can be compared with meaning in relation to language. It does not consist in simply feeling, but in what can be accomplished through feeling, just as it is meaning that lends significance to the words we use. Sexual love can include three essential human elements, the animal, the social—communal bond, and the internal spiritual bond. Any one of these elements is incomplete if it is isolated from the rest. Sex for its own sake, the exclusive preoccupation with social or family life and spiritual love that denies the flesh or that considers itself superior to the others—all such separation can lead to perversion. In fact it was the separation of these intrinsic elements in the Ireland of his times that caused Brian Merriman to pick up his pen in order to restore to society what was lacking of a basic, healthy, animal instinct, free of conventional guilt.

Animal Nature

The great Welsh poet/ novelist D.H. Lawrence went further than any writer of his time in his exploration of human sexuality. It is no wonder his books caused such unquiet and were so summarily banned. He carried forward the spirit of the Romantics who neglected the animal world and the sexual element in nature and tended to avoid the implications of animal instinct in humans. Including in his honest observation insects, fishes, birds, beasts, and flowers he affirms the grandeur, mystery and substance of our common life.

Poetry arises for Lawrence out of the immediacy of nature and woman. In *Love on the Farm* he shows us a man going into the house to embrace a woman. He has just caught a rabbit in a snare and is gently mindful of the woman's identification of herself with the trapped animal.

Through making room for all that we are in the fullness of our natural lives we can access and embody a connectedness with the world around us and with one another. Bodies can only meet unselfconsciously when we rejoice in the conditions of our own mortality and move through them into a deeper communion with the love that already permeates our souls.

>...and the world for one moment closed its terrifying eyes
> in gratitude
> Saying
> "This is my body, I am found."
>> From David Whyte, Fire In the Earth

Love and the Meeting of Bodies

The impression I retained from my earliest sexual escapades and some later ones as well was that Irish people could only permit themselves such licence when under the influence of alcohol, that the act was short-lived and much overrated as an activity, yielding little satisfaction for a woman. It was a long time before I learned that sobriety and skill on the part of the man, a complete absence of shame and a wide-awake conscious attention would be the means through which I would break the chain of repression to which I was heir.

> *I knew that one shouldn't hide the physical act of love any longer, because that game was repugnant. I knew we had to look at it differently simply to look at it. I prefer our manner today, accepting more readily our risks than the lies of the past, but love is in danger. I see clearly that it is in danger...*

Treasa O'Driscoll

This passage appears in a remarkable book by Jacques Lusseyran, who was born in Paris in 1924. Blind from the age of eight, he developed unparalleled capacities of inner seeing, which enabled him to experience images revelatory of the outside world. Robert Sardello, in his introduction to the book Lusseyran addressed to his wife, *Conversation Amoureuse*, points out that to move beyond his own subjective images the author had to free himself from all disruptive emotions such as fear, anger, jealousy and impatience and that he had to live the reality of love in full consciousness. This intensified his acuity of touch, hearing and smell considerably and allowed him to enter fully into a meditation on the mystery of love. This began to unfold within him in his teens and later deepened into a mature experience of marriage. Sardello, himself a pioneer of this phenomenological approach, has focused his own singular light on the subject and points out that:

> *A man dreams, not so much of the perfect woman, but of the luminous feminine, a dream that, for the most part exists only partly consciously. He desires the flesh and blood woman. And a woman, does she not experience the same division in counter fashion? Love has a hard time of it however, as long as dream and desire live a separate existence.*
> *From Robert Sardello*

I am of the opinion that women suffer more consistently for love than men. The satisfaction of desire in a man can be swiftly accomplished in the act of love but infatuation inflicts a slow torture of wanting-but-not-getting on a woman whose rational mind becomes for the time being impaired! I have tended towards infatuation, in love with love from a very early age. As I became more conscious I realized that this was a form of *self-feeling*, the anticipation of pleasure that the dream awakens in the body. It sometimes happens that when a man responds to these subtle mating signals he is rejected, because the reality of his ordinary flesh and blood nature, his lack of artifice and simple human need, can shock a woman out of her reverie. This scenario occurred in my life a few times making me aware of the dramas I was capable of activating. When I look back on the more unconscious period of my life I see how much I was enmeshed in the invisible entanglements of my own dream weaving. I am still learning to separate the subjective fantasy from the objective reality of the preferred other.

Nuala O'Faolain's novel *My Dream Of You,* brought this whole issue to point for me. A contemporary of my own and frequent participant in the Merriman school, Nuala has so internalized the wanting-but-not-getting syndrome that afflicts so many women, taking readers to the bottom of desire and longing with such uncompromising candor that her book is itself the antidote for the condition it presents. It is fortunate that Love does not ultimately depend on our intervention in drawing together those who are kindred at levels of body, soul and spirit and the great adventure of life is in allowing ourselves to be surprised by the divine fitness of what unfolds as in the case of O'Faolain's heroine.

We must be prepared to approach one another with the utmost purity of intent and mindful of the need to care and nourish the body and keep it healthy and fit. The man of my experience who was most profoundly and in an objective and subjective sense a lover, was alert in every nuance of the sexual act as he was in every other area of life. He helped me become aware of how deep rooted my habit of avoiding relationship was. I began to understand that the sexual act, when entered into with open eyes and a deep respect for the autonomy of the other, was something complete in itself and a means of becoming more authentic. I could release him from the dream without breaking a loving connection with him, able to love somebody at last for his own sake.

> *One touches Heaven when one touches the human body.*
> From Novalis, Fragments

Lusseyran has this to add:

> *The couple capable of listening to the least movement of these two bodies lent to them for love, this couple would break the chain and the souls would enter... But the condition is this yes given to the body, this all-inclusive yes.*

Was not this indeed the message James Joyce wanted to convey through Molly Bloom's memorable soliloquy, peppered with affirmatives, the part that most people remember of his novel Ulysses and the passage with which I often end my recitals:

> *...And then I asked him with my eyes to ask again yes and then he asked me would I yes to say yes my mountain flower and first I put my arms round him and drew him down to me so he could feel my breasts all perfume yes and his heart was going like mad and yes I said yes I will yes.*

Man and woman can navigate these crossings between dream and desire by bringing conscious attention into their every movement and gesture towards one another until the act takes on meditative rhythm. Hands must be allowed to function with the sensitivity of the artist. When we regard the nude figures sculpted by Rodin, for instance, we understand to what degree he had perfected a sense of touch. With earnest, solitary patience and with tireless hands this concentrated workman revealed mysteries of physical attraction. Rilke, who was (for a period) his secretary, remarks of *The Kiss... we feel as if waves were passing from all the surface contact points into their bodies, the thrill of beauty, of invitation and of power...* I think there is far more to be gained for the art of love-making and the development of inner sensitivity, in the study of such works than in the passive witnessing of the spectacles of copulation guaranteed today at the flick of a button, that ultimately numbs sensory imagination.

Finding What We Did not Lose

Lusseyran was imbued with an ideal of the feminine since age sixteen and when inwardly ready, he was inevitably 'found' by the flesh and blood woman whose existence he had fathomed.

> *For me that woman was already a being. She was somebody whose presence moved me, questioned me. She was a living person, fully formed... I could not have said where she was or when she would come. But I knew what she would demand from me... she was going to urge me on to live... She would finally draw out of me everything I contained.*

The woman who would embody this vocation would be self actualized. She would not yield to the temptation to make his life more important than hers. Love insists that we do not mistake another's destiny for our own, it being above all a path towards authenticity and communion. If the dream can ultimately lead the woman to love in the flesh, the man can let desire lead him through the sexual act to the actual source of that eternal feminine that lures him on. They will discover that there is a part of each of them that is already the other sex, each having penetrated through intimacy the experience of the other that goes beyond words. This brings the war between the sexes to its logical end and makes what Lusseyran terms *the new marriage* possible. The continual adaptation of two people to one another can be mirrored in the sexual act, a vital function of the relationship that deepens through dialogue and ever increasing interest in the other's well-being. Perhaps the most difficult task we have been given as human beings is that we should succeed in fully loving one other person for the other's own sake. So much are we preoccupied with the search for so-called soul mates, even in old age, that it would seem as Rilke has pointed out that it is the task *for which all other work is merely preparation...* Most blessed of all are those who in later life, after the necessities of family life have been satisfied, find or rediscover a kindred other with whom to share a common task.

Unlike the man, whose sex is local and genital, the woman's sexuality is diffused throughout her body and in less enlightened times it usually happened that she was just warming up when the man was already finished. Her fundamental giving of herself is deeply emotional in contrast to the man's more immediately physical expression. Both experience at different levels a giving of the self which transcends any gradable comparison. Lusseyran could observe how desire begins to take hold of a woman and bring about physical change.

> *She has received from us everything that we held until that moment of available life... she becomes change,... she becomes everything of which the universe is capable.*

Yet for thousands of years women around the world have lived and died without experiencing the great natural gift of orgasm. And it is within the power of a man to awaken this capacity in a woman for which she can feel nothing but the deepest gratitude and which makes her belong with him in a totally genuine way. This energetic exchange can be the source of a true harmony and rhythm and trust in the life of a couple. For every action we perform to its completion, helps to free us from compulsion and dissatisfaction. By being totally engaged in an act of love we become free of the co-dependency that is often associated with sexual needs.

The restraint involved in conscious loving, the activity of sensory awareness it demands, the attentiveness to mutuality, timing and shifting moods is often enhanced by periods of celibacy, of natural withdrawal and regeneration. It is a path of discovery for which each couple must chart their own course. It will advance as we shape the love between the sexes into a more conscious relation of one human being to another and extend more loving interest towards the members of our own sex.

The modern man and woman is responsible for the future of love, of love-making as process, because there is creativity involved in increasing the presence of love in the world. Making room for bodies and souls to cohere in the same earthly dimension can only occur when we bring consciousness to bear in the endeavour. This brings an inexorable flow of grace and harmony into our lives, and advances Rilke's vision of *the love that consists in this— that two solitudes protect and border and greet each other.*

Treasa O'Driscoll

> *The first step to a qualitative, further development of consciousness is a formation of a consciousness of the present, in which one no longer needs to rely on the contents of the past in order to stay awake, but can say, out of the experience of the present, I am.*
> Georg Kühlewind

Twelve

A SENSE OF RENEWAL

Georg Kühlewind's words didn't impact my life overnight. In truth, it has taken me a lifetime of experience, study, inspiration and, above all, the example of others whom I deeply respect. Dr. Ross Laing introduced me to what he referred to as *truthing*, the process of bringing what is hidden to light, of attentiveness to the actual state of heart behind the words we utter. There is often an implicit agreement between people to support and harbor each other's dishonesties and repressions. This protects them from having to change habits or lifestyle. Making a change requires a shift in consciousness, a willingness to become more conscious in what one thinks and says and does. The possibility of new beginnings arise when authenticity is sustained in our interactions, when words carry weight between people. Fears, needs and fixed positions fall away when the light of understanding is shone into the darkness of confused emotions. *Perceiving the light awakens love of the light, of the truth which distinguishes itself from all darker manifestations... It awakens love which does not yet exist, in order that it might become...* states Dr Kühlewind. What was remarkable about my experience with Ross was that this adventure in *truthing* was conducted in the presence of many other people and suggestive of a new direction in community living. By the grace of truth, something can manifest in each moment, a new cycle of love is initiated which owes nothing to tradition, ritual or myth only to the very fact of being wholly present to one's environment.

Dr. Kühlewind points out that the new love is not concerned with requital and is therefore not overtly concerned with sex. Decadent forms of sexuality are those which are not free because they are not conscious, he believes. Without diminishing pleasure, sex can become a free, conscious act, a function of authentic relationship, a celebration of the sacred mystery of love. While we are overwhelmed by reminders of how great the rift between the sexes is, for some time now the conversation of love has been moving in a new direction. If rapport on a spiritual and soul level has not been established between partners before they embark on their physical mating their communication skills may prove inadequate when romance begins to wane. Love for the other's own sake and love beyond desire is the actual, realizable goal of earthly love. To achieve this goal it is essential for couples to engage in a form of dialogue with one another that keeps them on the creative edge, daring to question assumptions that together they take courage in exploding. It is the nitty gritty of soul work that brings about the transformation of feelings and thought content.

The majority of people I saw turning up at the *Toronto Institute of Self Healing* were seeking to stimulate channels of communication that had dried up between partners. It seemed to me that men and women operate on different levels and it is useful to recognize this from the outset. A common story about a pair who had been dating for six months serves to illustrate these differences. The woman thought it was time they discussed their future plans... Driving home one night after an enjoyable dinner she decided to broach the topic.

"John, do you realize that we have been dating since last October and that we have seen each other three nights of every week on average....?"

"Really darling," he responded. "Has it been that long? Ah yes, I remember now! I met you when I had just had my car repaired. The carburetor and alternator had given up on the very same day! Such inconvenience! You know I have never been fully satisfied with this car..."

He continued his discourse on this favorite topic of his until it was time to drop her off at her address, and he wondered why she slammed the door. He went home slightly perplexed, but slept soundly. She meanwhile burst into tears as soon as her roommate appeared and launched into a litany of complaint about the insensitivity of men... Before a couple can get beyond this tug-of-war it is necessary to recognize the impetuous reactions that block authentic dialogue. What is automatic is never conscious.

Now that men and women are becoming equal from the point of view of education and career, the old role playing formulas can no longer be sustained. Both are breadwinners, both have interests outside the home, both travel, both have their own friends. A new order is called for in which relationships will not deteriorate into entanglements. Central to the work of Ross Laing and his wife Andrea and their co-directors at the Institute, Dermot and Fran Grove-White, is the creation of the new model of relationship they exemplify. I attended several of their couple groups in which partners were encouraged to really listen to one another and witness the contrasting modalities through which they function, coming to clearer perspective of the other's point of view. Participants were encouraged to approach one another with honesty, vulnerability and a willingness to accept responsibility for creating the relationship they had. The current of love generated in these sessions was awesome.

When, a few years later, Claude would initiate a conversation with the words: "Let's not just talk about what we know, but remain open to what we don't know," I could sense the approach of an eternal moment, a qualitative deepening of the love we shared

> *The Logos connects human beings through the Word—*
> *all else is temptation or a temporary connection. To*
> *look for the connecting element elsewhere is to*
> *disregard the new commandment.*
> *From Kühlewind*

Love reveals itself in this new millennium as a light in thinking, a torch the poets I have quoted throughout this book, have always held aloft, a thinking now available to everyone. It is a thinking that owes nothing to the past, the thinking that Claude characterized when he described thoughts as "something active, living, the working forces of the world ...something cosmic, divine." Although he did not know it, his statement echoes a definition given by Rudolf Steiner. Electricity, Dr. Steiner contended is comparable to human thought. The relationship that ice cubes have to water, physical atoms have to the flow of electricity, and our formations of finished thoughts have to the more fluid stream of living intuitive thinking. As imprisoned light, each atom in the universe bears within one of its minute parts, a microcosmic likeness of what will emerge in future creation.

Spirit is continually slipping into the atom and this atom holds the image of the future plan, just as intuition enlivens thinking as inspiration, invention and imagination bringing new growth and creativity into the world. Our electric currents of thought affect everything in our atmosphere and have a direct bearing on what will unfold in our lives, most particularly in the condition of our own health and destiny. When creative dialogue is allowed to flourish between friends and lovers new expressions of human harmony and cooperation enter the fray of life, a force for social renewal.

True Meetings

Behind the desire to love and be loved, is a basic human aspiration to see and be seen. If we see one another only in terms of outer behavior and the appearance of wealth, status, deprivation, or fixed identity of color, class or creed, we miss the experience of the essential humanity of another. For each of us is a living, changing organism in which the whole of creation is reflected. The conductor of this symphonic interplay of material and spiritual forces is the unique 'I' being or *Self* that we can learn to recognize in one another. People sometimes take a limited view of themselves, succumbing to the circumstances of the moment; *I am hopeless, I am awkward, I am alcoholic, I am depressed*, does not define the whole person. Inherent in the syntax of the Irish language is the concept of the passing nature of attributes and possessions. We say *tá sé agam*—it is *at* me, denoting the presence of something in my vicinity, but not my identity with it. The first instance of the practice of forgiveness in our lives surely arises in relation to ourselves. We stumble less through trial and error, find less to forgive in ourselves the more we gain perspective of the conditions of our lives. Once when I was going through a period of turmoil, a friend gave me a postcard of the heavens. An arrow pointed towards the tiny dot that represented our earth among a cluster of galaxies. The caption read *You are HERE!*

While each one may be small in the large physical scheme of things, one's individual presence is of immeasurable value to the well-being of the whole. I view each self as a living culture, engaged in a vital exchange with the surrounding environment. To be spiritually discerning is to realize a deep sense of purpose in life and give thanks for the awesome evolutionary means that lie at our disposal. Everything that emanates from us or which impinges on us from outside, occurs by grace of the senses, our bridge from inner to outer awareness. Rudolf Steiner called the senses wellsprings of the soul.

He numbered them twelve, contrary to the popular consensus of five. When we refer to our *sixth sense* we often mean one or other of the seven additional senses Steiner identified. The first eight, designated *lower* and *middle* senses are the following: Touch, Life, Movement, Balance, Smell, Taste, Sight and Warmth; these relate to body and soul faculties. The other four termed by Steiner the spiritual senses can be juxtaposed with the four bodily senses of touch, life, movement and balance. The more effectively these latter four are developed in early childhood the more likely we are to have the spiritual senses strengthened in us in later life, those of Hearing, Concept, Language and 'I' sense. I recently experienced a deeper understanding of this latter sense when I visited the Goetheanum in Switzerland. The majestic building which towers above the town of Dornach, houses an enormous wooden sculpture that Rudolf Steiner carved to near completion during his final years on earth. Entitled *The Representative of Man*, it features a lone figure standing against a background of opposing forces. Emanating nobility and poise, one hand raises upwards, the other points below, in the eurythmic gesture for the German *Ich*. It signified for me the continual momentum of the Christ's redeeming presence in every human soul, the living reality of *Not I, but Christ in me*, holding the promise of our full humanity in the face of all adversity.

In the meeting between two people there is a kind of subtle non-physical touching going on. We tend to scan for the impression of the essential being of the person we meet, which is a kind of 'force form'. Making contact with other people entails the proper functioning of our senses of language, thought and 'I'. The latter is perhaps the most elusive of all the senses but I believe it is the one most important to cultivate in the twenty-first century. The renewal of social life depends on it. Steiner did not mean by the 'I' sense that you bolster your own ego but that you become aware of somebody else as an 'I', looking past surface impressions to what is truly individual in the other.

Through this sense we pay attention to *who* is speaking more than to *what* is said. In this way we move from the experience of one another's behavior to experiencing the actual experience of the other.

The more genuine the expression, the more clearly the individuality of the other can be seen. This is true for everyone. When a speaker stands behind his words you know you can count on that person to follow through in action. Too often people fail us in this respect. Promises made in the heat of the moment often fail to engage the will of the speaker and are quickly forgotten. To build trust in oneself and others words must be binding, active agents of responsibility. The 'I' sense that is present in everyone is under attack whenever a person suffers from an addiction. The bridge that this sense can build between people is always undermined by drugs or alcohol. While under their influence, we become unreachable by others and we lose the ability to penetrate through to the 'I' of another. This tragedy of isolation gives rise to the despair suffered by addicts. The manic-depressive syndrome also produces this distressing effect in both the sufferer and the care-giver. Rather than accept this limitation we must redouble our efforts to reach those who seem most remote from us. This effort can be developed on the inner plane and always proves effective in the long run. When one of my sons was going through his period of teenage rebellion, he entered the danger zone of drugs, then readily available on the streets of Toronto. I was beside myself with worry, powerless I thought, in the face of the collective peer pressure to which he was subject. It was as if I had lost all connection with him. John Davy was visiting at the time and he gave me the best advice I ever received as a parent.

"You have had a sense since birth, have you not," John said, "of your child's unique spiritual presence? Regardless of his behavior at present you must concentrate on always seeing this light in him and gradually you will call it forth into expression. His 'I' forces are not yet strong because he is under twenty-one. You must help sustain them for him."

I have employed this technique of holding my children in light, throughout all the viccissitudes of growth and I recommend it to other troubled parents.

The New Sense

The most creative forms of dialogue unfold for those who start out from a common set of assumptions they have freely reached. When not at odds about the fundamental nature and purpose of life, companions can enter into a mutual exploration of the truth. Lady Gregory's remark about John Millington Synge comes to mind. "I do not have to rearrange my mind to talk to him." Consider, how rare and wonderful this privilege might be in a world where we seem to be explaining ourselves always in the effort to be understood.

I enjoy fruitful dialogue with a young monk who holds a similar frame of reference to mine. I always depart our brief but satisfying exchanges full of a sense of having seen and been seen in the essential self. This experience constitutes what we call in Irish *anam-cáirdeas*, soul friendship. *A soul without a friend*, we say, *is like a body without a head.* My friend used to work as a psychotherapist before joining a religious order. He possesses a unique clairvoyant gift, the result of eyes washed clean of self-seeking, which enables him to apprehend the light body of the person he sees before him.

He asked me one day to consider, what the purpose of this capacity might be and whether he should allow it to develop further. My intuitive response to his question was—"Be grateful for this gift. Even if the person is not aware that you are seeing him in the aspect of color and light, your very act of perception will affirm his sense of self worth. This true foundation of being is overlooked, or only of passing interest, to many today. People need confirmation of the innate purity and goodness of their essential makeup, no matter how much contamination has occurred on other levels in the course of their lives."

As I drove away from the monastery that day I thought of the amount of therapy it takes to overcome the so-called ego. Yet the surest method and the one most likely to assist in the process of spiritualizing the earth is our attempt to see others as existing out of the same fullness of importance that we assign to ourselves.

My most enduring friendships are with those rare individuals to whom my mind needs no adjustment. Their understanding of my concerns is implicit because of an accord that is natural between us. Anne Stockton is one such cherished friend and mentor. A gifted painter, born in New York in 1910, she has lived through most of the twentieth century, founding the Tobias School for art therapy in England in the early seventies. Anne is a woman of great natural beauty and refined intellect, her soul imbued with the qualities of the colors that illumine her work. She shines in every surrounding, a charismatic center of wit and wisdom. To be in her company is to experience the warmth of yellow, the dynamism of red, the kindness of blue and the fertile newness of green. Memory lapse is not a feature of Anne's old age. She has an endearing ability in

Treasa O'Driscoll

conversation to remain focused on a theme until it has been exhausted to our mutual satisfaction. While we give one another license to wander off into imaginative tangents, she invariably holds the thread. She has honed this facility in her lifelong practice of the color and concentration exercises given by Rudolf Steiner. This schooling in attention makes her fully present in each moment with a delightful childlike curiosity so that young people are drawn to her wherever she is. She is the oldest in years of the people I love most. I readily responded to her invitation to spend the last days of the century with her in Dornach, Switzerland. We raised our glasses in a toast to the New Year after attending a performance of Beethoven's ninth symphony at the Goetheanum. She characteristically declared: "My dear, when a thought pops into my head from now on, I shall ask myself 'Is this idea of the new millennium or of the old?' because new ideas must always be allowed to come forth and one must guard against resting on one's laurels." In my favorite photograph of Anne she is leaning against the ancient oak tree that shades my writer's cottage, a fitting backdrop for one whose eyes reflect the wisdom of the age.

Mercy for the Trees

When I returned to County Clare to put the finishing touches to this book, a pile of Christmas mail awaited me. The first letter I opened bore a British Columbia postmark, turning my thoughts to Canada once again. I recognized the handwriting of a cherished friend, Glada McIntyre. She wrote:

> *We are wrapped in the cloak of winter today. When snow is falling the outside world seems far away. How we cherish these peaceful winter months hidden away on the mountain top. We have all the*

food and supplies we need till Spring, as we have had for the past 20 winters here... It keeps one wonderfully in tune with the profound light of the natural earth, going to the spring for water, grinding grain every day for our bread, fuelling the fire, feeding the animals, milking the cow and making yoghurt and butter, preparing the meals from all the delicious living food we are so fortunate to be able to grow. One just takes for granted that the days are filled with contemplation and prayer - the almost subconscious invocation on lighting the morning candle, or the evening lamps. This was not common practice in the culture I grew up in, though I think it was in yours - the interaction, in reverence, with the elements - the sacred earth, the sacred fire, the sacred water, the sacred air...

I first met Glada on a warm Sunday morning in August 1995. She happened to enter a hall where I was singing and recognized my voice as one she had heard on Canadian radio several years before. We established an immediate rapport. Two of my sons were with me. Later as we sat outside in the glorious sunshine a horse drawn wagon driven by an imposing bearded man pulled up and we were soon lumbering up a forest trail, holding on for dear life. The location was Argenta, a remote outlying region beyond the town of Nelson, not identified on the map. I had driven for fifteen hours up the mountains from Vancouver at the behest of my son Declan. Along the way Vince, Glada's Irish-born husband, pointed towards their grazing Kerry cows.

"Two of the last two-hundred remaining of that species in the world. The calf was produced from semen sent over from Ireland." There was still a trace of his accent.

I noticed patches of vegetables and colorful clusters of flowers as we gingerly alighted, to make our way along a mossy path to the clearing they had appropriated many years before, and could now claim as their own property.

"We grow organic vegetables in fields spread out across various locations on the mountainside and sell them throughout the region," Vince continued.

"At first we dug a hole to preserve root vegetables, then added a glass dome. Soon we had built ourselves a temporary shelter which, in the course of time, became our home," Glada added. She pulled open a door to the most unusual house I had ever entered—more like the inside of a tree. Only the imagination of a Tolkien could stretch to a fitting description. It was a dwelling hospitable to elemental beings. No running water or electricity, and yet all their domestic needs were ingeniously met... I looked enviously into their storeroom. There was an abundance of canned peaches, tomatoes, plums, apricots, huckleberry jam, homemade cheese and yoghurt. A hearty meal of delicious pancakes was set before us, dripping with freshly churned butter and syrup. A sturdy gas stove was all Glada had to rely on in producing her nutritious breads and pies, and there was a seemingly endless supply of piping hot organic tea. I asked Glada why there had been such a stir when she entered the hall.

"I was singing, but all heads turned in your direction!" I joked.

"I think it is because of the *Singing Forest*" she said "I am well known in the area because of it."

"Do tell me more" I said.

A woman of forty odd years, she stood before us in luminous beauty, framed by the walls of windowed glass in this special sanctuary among the trees.

"I will tell you about a remarkable experience I had on the 15th of June 1990. Vince and I and our crew of treeplanters were at work up Howser Creek, in the Purcell mountains. We were only making 20 cents a tree. It was tough going, mashed woody debris paved into hardpan down on the flat by the creek, and dense yew brush on a fairly steep slope above; a long run to treeline, but not many opportunities to stick in a tree."

"I stood up to stretch. I saw a beam of light ray out from a mountain named the Virgin, over the nearby forest. As my attention was drawn to the illuminated trees, I was struck by their immense verticality. A profound vertical alignment took place in me in response. Suddenly I felt about twelve feet tall. Then I was struck in my solar plexus by an impact of sound. It grew into a swelling, crescendoing symphony, in range and tone unlike anything I had heard before! Emanating from the forested hillsides across the valley, it was unquestionably a hymn of adoration, of joy in creation and praise to the creator! Words cannot possibly express the magnitude of this joyous sound, nor my absolute joy in hearing it."

We listened enthralled. Glada's eyes began to glisten as she continued:

"Tears were streaming down my face, I know that my whole life had led up to this revelation, this was why I had studied forest ecology, had sought out visionary teachers. This is what I was seeking, the underlying reality. This I knew, is why I have always chosen to live and work in the forest."

Vince interjected "I remember the day so well and the profound way in which Glada was affected. She kept asking me 'Do you hear it?' asking others 'Can you hear?' But only she could hear."

A darker note entered Glada's narrative. "I was revelling in the immensity of the experience. I was washed clean, flooded with joy and strength and awe. Then suddenly the song changed. It was an abrupt change from overwhelming joy to abject sorrow. My cognitive mental faculty was being given a new urgent message. If I could put words to it..., "it would be this." She paused for breath:

OH NOBLE AND WORTHY EXPLOITERS AND CONQUERORS

HAVE MERCY. HAVE MERCY. DO NOT END OUR SINGING WHICH ALLOWS THE CONDITIONS NECESSARY

FOR ALL LIFE ON THE PLANET AS YOU KNOW IT!"

My son Declan leaned closer to me, "The trees in the *Singing Forest* in Tenise Creek are one thousand years old!"

Glada continued. "I was haunted by that litany for months, awakening to its echo in the night: Have mercy, Have mercy on the children."

Vince interjected, "She was given a great deal of information almost instantaneously which totally altered the direction of our lives. Since then Glada has been tireless in her efforts to stop the logging. Many people have joined in her campaign, but we are up against the forces of capitalism."

"I received a number of vivid impressions during this clairaudient revelation," Glada continued. "I know now that the biggest, oldest trees receive broadcast of life force energy from the inner regions in the vicinity of the valley's headwaters, and that these ancient beings transform and transmit that life-renewing energy throughout the entire ecosystem and that when they are removed, the ecosystem is plunged into chaos, within which biotic succession is not predictable."

Her face brightening again to its customary glow. "The *Singing Forest* is sacred to the divine spirit of grace and mercy represented in the East by Kwan Yin, in the West she is called Mary, Holy Mother, or Sophia."

Briain was obviously moved. He looked at me and said, "I think I will remain here with Glada and Vince. They may need help with the harvest or with their work in spreading news of the forest." Then remembering himself he shyly asked, "That is if they would like me to stay?" The look on their faces gave instant affirmation. Thus began an interesting period for him living in their adjacent cabin and working with them daily he established a life-long friendship with two remarkable people.

Glada shared another insight with us during that first meeting concerning the Yggdrasil tree.

"It represents a sacred place created by the Gods, from whence all life is sustained. There is a clear connection for me between this Viking legend and the revelation of the *Singing Forest.*"

Declan, then aged twenty, subsequently also settled near the McIntyre's and often visited them. Glada became a mentor for him, he took up the study of Icelandic mythology. He found an old map, printed in 1890, that identified neighboring mountains, all bearing names associated with Icelandic lore. In the same spirit with which Yeats restored old stories to popular consciousness, Declan set to writing a play that would give local people new imaginative connection with the majestic ranges that surrounded them. A multimedia production entitled *Shadow of the Yggdrasil* was soon in rehearsal in Nelson. Seventy young people played their part in this brave cooperative endeavour, either on stage or off, with Declan conducting operations while also taking the part of Baldur in the show.

Soon after reading Glada's letter, I received the following summons from Nelson—*Mom, please come to Nelson. The play is opening on February 9th. I have written you into a scene. You must come!*

How could I refuse? I made the arduous journey across a continent to the furthest northern point, arriving only minutes before the final rehearsal. Declan hailed me from a company of lavishly costumed Gods and Godesses.

"Oh good! You're here. Can you come on stage? Baldur is just about to die and I want you to sing a keen over the body."

Jet-lag notwithstanding, I hastened to obey the Sun God's command! Next evening I sat with Vince and Glada in the theatre and gave thanks with them for inspiration well received. The night's audience were rising in a standing ovation.

Then it was back to Tinarana House to the steadily rising pile of pages. The book was nearing its end. That end signalled another beginning.

Shortly after returning I began to prepare for a conference of the *School of Spiritual Psychology* at the nearby Glenstal Abbey. This was the fulfillment of an eager wish to facilitate a gathering of North American friends in Ireland. As one participant later remarked, "Here we have a meeting of opportunity and hospitality." Opportunity is the hallmark of American incentive, while the tradition of hospitality in Irish monasteries is legendary, and was entirely upheld on this occasion. Our theme for the event was *The Healing Field of the Soul*. A confluence of tributaries representing

Spiritual Psychology, Irish monasticism, Anthroposophy, and Mysticism, duly converged on Glenstal.

Maybe we shall know each other better
When the tunnels meet beneath the mountain.
From Louis Macniece

Brother Mark Patrick Hederman quoted these lines at the opening of the conference. Remarking that no meeting takes place by chance, he said, "It was meant to be, and has only come to be, because a number of historical—cultural circumstances have cleared it's way..."

Mark Patrick is a Glenstal monk, a philosopher who carries a clear vision for the social renewal that is possible when Ireland faces its own peculiar darkness. Consciousness soul shines through every gesture and word of this contemporary poet.

Wonder and enquiry stirred our minds and hearts throughout those days and strengthened the soul forces of all present. White robed monks made their procession towards the altar several times a day, forming a reverent circle with outstretched hands, when the host was raised above the chalice.

"They remind me of the Grail Brotherhood," remarked Anne, who knelt beside me.

I gave thanks. The adventure of my year in Ireland had come full circle. My new book would speak an echoing voice that reverberated in the meeting of these complimentary streams of knowledge and wisdom, the formative substance of my thinking and writing.

The thought came to me. It was Irish druids who first began the work of opening human hearts to the mystery of love, often in monastic settings like this one. The continuation of this task still remains a living purpose on this small island at the windswept edge of Europe. The continuity of spiritual tradition within Irish monasticism was enlivened in this encounter, with connected offshoots of a common Christian root.

I looked around at the faces of my friends, some new some of a lifetime. They were assembled in a farewell circle on the monastery green on the last day. These men and women devote their lives to the task of awakening hearts with their writings, teachings, meditation and clinical practices.

It was indeed a motley crew of monks, minstrels, scholars, artists, jacks-of-all-trades, who were gathered with me from near and far. A red rose passed around the gathering from hand to hand.

When it was my turn, I gave thanks. Thanks for the ideas and memories shared in my fledgling writing; thanks for the warm convergence of kindred spirits.

I am astonished at the glory of friendship. A friendship shared with such a diversity of people across continents and years. I am heartened by this love between friends that forms a radiant circle round every heart, rippling out into halos of stars that merge and glow above the roads we travel.

The End

BIBLIOGRAPHY

Balough, Teresa. May Human Beings Hear It., Circle Publishers

Bradley, Ian. The Celtic Way, Darton, Longman and Todd

Brown, Paula. The New Mary, in Ariadne's Awakening, ed. Margli Matthews, Hawthorn Press

Carmichael, Alexander. The Sun Dances: Prayers and Blessings from the Gaelic, Floris Books, 1997

Cronin, Anthony. Samuel Beckett: The Last Modernist, Harper Collins, 1997

Cortto, Jeremy. Mysticism, Aquarian Press

Davy, John. Hope, Evolution and Change, Anthroposophic Press, 1990

De Fréine, Seán. The Great Silence, Mercier Press, 1994

Eliot, T.S. Collected Poems, 1909-1962, Harcourt Brace, 1963

Fitzgerald, Astrid. The Artist's Book of Inspiration, Anthroposophic Press, 1996

Flower, Robin. The Irish Tradition, Oxford Univ Press, Dufour Editions

Heaney, Seamus. The Redress of Poetry, Faber and Faber, 1996

Heaney, Seamus. Opened Ground, Selected Poems 1966-1996, Faber & Faber

Hederman, Mark Patrick. Kissing the Dark, Veritas, 1999

Hillman, James, Michael Meade, and Robert Bly, eds. The Rag & Bone Shop of the Heart, Harperperennial, 1993

Hull, Eleanor. Cuchulainn, George & Harrap Co, 1913

Kühlewind, Georg. Becoming Aware of the Logos, Lindisfarne Books, 1984

Kühlewind, Georg. From Normal to Healthy, Lindisfarne Books, 1988

Laing, R.D. Knots, Random House, 1972

Lawrence, D.H. Complete Poems, Penguin Books, 1994

Lusseryan, Jacques. Conversation Amourese, introduction by Robert Sardello, Rudolf Steiner College Press

Matthews, Paul. Sing Me the Creation, Anthroposophic Pr, 1996

O'Connor, Frank. Kings, Lord and Commons, MacMillan & Co, 1962

O'Driscoll, Robert. The Celtic Consciousness, George Braziller Press, 1990

O Muirithe, Diarmuid. A Seat Behind The Coachman, Gill and Macmillan

Osho, Rajneesh. Tantric Transformation, Element, 1994

Raine, Kathleen. Selected Poems, Inner Traditions/Lindisfarne Press, 1988

Redfield, James. The Tenth Insight, Warner Books, 1998

Rilke, Rainer Maria. Selected Poems, Trans. Robert Bly, Harper & Row, 1988

Rilke, Rainer Maria. Rodin and Other Prose Pieces, Quartet Books

Rilke, Rainer Maria. Duino Elegies, Trans. David Young, W.W. Norton & Co, 1978

Sardello, Robert. Freeing the Soul From Fear, Riverhead Books, 1999

Sardello, Robert. Love and the Soul: Creating a Future for the Earth, Harper Collins, 1995

Soesman, Albert. Our Twelve Senses, Hawthorn Press, 1990

Solovyov, Vladimir. The Meaning of Love, Lindisfarne Books, 1989

Steiner, Rudolf. Occult Science-An Outline, Anthroposophic Press, 1972

Steiner, Rudolf. The Fifth Gospel, Rudolf Steiner Press

Steiner, Rudolf. Cosmic Memory: Prehistory of Earth and Man, Lindisfarne Books, 1990

Steiner, Rudolf. Love and its Meaning in the World, Rudolf Steiner Press,

Stephens, James. Irish Fairy Tales, Dover Pub, 1996

Sussman, Linda. The Speech of the Grail, Lindisfarne Books, 1997

Walshe, M.O. Meister Eckhart: Sermons and Treatises, Element Books

Whyte, David. Fire in the Earth, Many Rivers Press, 1997

Wordsworth, William. John O. Hayden, ed., William Wordsworth: Selected Poems, Penguin Classics, 1994

Yeats, W.B. The Collected Poems, Macmillan, 1974

Zeldin, Theodore. Conversation, The Harvill Press

Printed in the United States
23293LVS00001B/7-57